First World War
and Army of Occupation
War Diary
France, Belgium and Germany

62 DIVISION
186 Infantry Brigade
213 Machine Gun Company
1 March 1917 - 28 February 1918

WO95/3087/4

The Naval & Military Press Ltd
www.nmarchive.com
Published in association with The National Archives

Published by

The Naval & Military Press Ltd

Unit 10 Ridgewood Industrial Park,

Uckfield, East Sussex,

TN22 5QE England

Tel: +44 (0) 1825 749494

www.naval-military-press.com

www.nmarchive.com

This diary has been reprinted in facsimile from the original. Any imperfections are inevitably reproduced and the quality may fall short of modern type and cartographic standards.

© **Crown Copyright**
Images reproduced by permission of The National Archives, London, England, 2015.

Contents

Document type	Place/Title	Date From	Date To
Heading	WO95/3087-4		
War Diary		01/11/1917	24/11/1917
Heading	62nd Division 186th Infy Bde 213th Machine Gun Coy Mar 1917-Feb 1918		
Heading	War Diary 213 Machine Gun Coy 186th Inf. Bde. From March 1. 1917 To March 31. 1917 Vol 1		
War Diary	Deepcut	01/03/1917	01/03/1917
War Diary	Southampton	01/03/1917	01/03/1917
War Diary	Havre	02/03/1917	07/03/1917
War Diary	Ascheux	08/03/1917	08/03/1917
War Diary	Englebelmer	09/03/1917	18/03/1917
War Diary	Miraumont	19/03/1917	22/03/1917
War Diary	Achiet Le Gd.	23/03/1917	26/03/1917
War Diary	G 6b Central (57 C)	27/03/1917	31/03/1917
Map	Machine Gun Position on the 62nd Division Front		
Heading	War Diary of 213 Coy M.G.C. From 1st April 1917 To 30th April 1917 Volume 2		
War Diary	G 6b Central Ref 57 C	01/04/1917	08/04/1917
War Diary	Mory	09/04/1917	18/04/1917
War Diary	B 28a 00	19/04/1917	30/04/1917
Heading	War Diary of 213th Machine Gun Company From 1st May 1917 To 31st May 1917 Volume 3		
War Diary	B 28a 00 (57c N.W)	01/05/1917	14/05/1917
War Diary	B7c72 (57c N.W)	15/05/1917	16/05/1917
War Diary	B15b 23 (57c N.W)	17/05/1917	19/05/1917
War Diary	A1b C 68 (57 C N.W)	20/05/1917	27/05/1917
Map	Ecoust-St. Mein		
Heading	Appendix No. 1 War Diary 213 Mg Coy Map Ecoust St. Mein 1/10,000		
War Diary	A 16 C 6.8 (57c N.W)	28/05/1917	29/05/1917
War Diary	B27 D.1.8 (57c N.W)	30/05/1917	31/05/1917
Heading	Appendix No.2 War Diary 213 Mg Coy Operation Order and Amendments Attack on Hindenburg Line 3.5.17		
Operation(al) Order(s)	213 Machine Gun Coy. Operation Order No.1	16/04/1917	16/04/1917
Miscellaneous	Amendments to 213 M.G. Coy Operation Order No.1	21/04/1917	21/04/1917
Map	Ecoust-St. Mein		
Heading	Appendix No.1 War Diary 213 Mg Coy Map Ecoust. St. Mein 1/10,000		
Heading	War Diary of 213 Coy M.G. C. From 1st June 1917 To 30th June 1917 Volume 4		
War Diary	B 28 B 45 (57c N.W)	01/06/1917	10/06/1917
War Diary	Achiet Le Petit	11/06/1917	26/06/1917
War Diary	C16b 12 (57c N.W)	27/06/1917	30/06/1917
Heading	War Diary of 213 Coy M.G.C. From 1/7/17 To 31/7/17 Volume 5		
War Diary	C 16b 12 (Ref.57c N.W)	01/07/1917	05/07/1917
War Diary	H 18d (ref 57c N.W)	05/07/1917	12/07/1917
War Diary	C22d80	13/07/1917	29/07/1917
War Diary	H 18a	30/07/1917	31/07/1917

Miscellaneous	213 M.G Coy Orders For Relief	12/07/1917	12/07/1917
Miscellaneous	Relief Order 213 M.G. Coy	11/07/1917	11/07/1917
Miscellaneous	Operation Order 213 M.G. Coy	16/07/1917	16/07/1917
Miscellaneous	Relief Order 213 M.G. Coy	23/07/1917	23/07/1917
Map	Ecoust-St. Mein		
Heading	Appendix No.1 War Diary 213 Mg. Coy Map Ecoust St. Mein 1/10,000		
Heading	War Diary of 213th Machine Gun Company From 1st August 1917 To 31st August 1917 Volume 6		
War Diary	H18a 57c N.W.	01/08/1917	02/08/1917
War Diary	C16b 12 57c N. W.	03/08/1917	11/08/1917
War Diary	H18a 57c N. W.	12/08/1917	19/08/1917
War Diary	B17b 57c N.W.	20/08/1917	31/08/1917
Map	Map I		
Heading	To Be Put With Diary Of 213 Coy. For August 1917		
Operation(al) Order(s)	Operation Order R 45 213 M.G. Coy	02/08/1917	02/08/1917
Heading	213 M.G. Coy War Diary Aug 1-31 1917		
Operation(al) Order(s)	Operation Order No.R. H 6 213 Machine Gun Coy		
Heading	213 M.G. Coy War Diary Aug 1-31.1917		
Miscellaneous	213 M.G. Coy Operation Order No.10		
Miscellaneous	Operation Order By Lieut R.H. Joyce Commanding 213th M.G Coy		
Heading	213 M.G. Coy War Diary Aug 1st-31st 1917		
Heading	War Diary of 213th M.G. Coy From 1st Sept 1917 To Sept 1917 Volume 7		
War Diary	B17b Central	01/09/1917	04/09/1917
War Diary	H18a Central	05/09/1917	15/09/1917
War Diary	Noreuil	16/09/1917	30/09/1917
Heading	213th M.G. Coy Appendix No 1 September 1917		
Miscellaneous	Operation Order By Capt. R.H. Joyce Commanding 213th M.G. Coy No. R 47		
Heading	213th M.G. Coy Appendix No.2 September 1917		
Operation(al) Order(s)	213th Machine Gun Company Operation Order No. 9	04/09/1917	04/09/1917
Heading	213th M.G. Coy Appendix No.3 September 1917		
Operation(al) Order(s)	213th Machine Gun Company Operation Order No.10	27/09/1917	27/09/1917
Heading	213th M.G. Coy Appendix No 4 September 1917		
Miscellaneous	Training Programme 213th M.G Coy		
Heading	213th M.G. Coy Appendix No.5 September 1917		
Miscellaneous	Company Routine Orders by Capt. L. Pollak Commanding 213th M.G. Company	19/09/1917	19/09/1917
Miscellaneous	Company Routine Orders by Capt. L.A. Pollak Cmdg. 213th M.G. Company	22/09/1917	22/09/1917
Heading	War Diary of 213th Machine Gun Coy. From 1st October 1917 To 31st October 1917 Volume 8		
War Diary	Beugnatre	01/10/1917	06/10/1917
War Diary	Noreuil	07/10/1917	09/10/1917
War Diary	Beugnatre	10/10/1917	12/10/1917
War Diary	Beulencourt	13/10/1917	30/10/1917
War Diary	Gomiecourt	31/10/1917	31/10/1917
Heading	213th M.G. Coy Appendix No. 1 October 1917		
Operation(al) Order(s)	213th Machine Gun Company Operation Order No.11	05/10/1917	05/10/1917
Miscellaneous	Table Of Relief		
Heading	213th M.G. Coy Appendix No.2 October 1917		
Operation(al) Order(s)	213th M.G. Coy Operation Order No. 12	08/10/1917	08/10/1917
Miscellaneous	Table Of Relief		
Heading	213th M.G. Coy Appendix No.3 October 1917		

Type	Description	Date From	Date To
Operation(al) Order(s)	213th Machine Gun Company Operation Order No. 13	29/10/1917	29/10/1917
Heading	213th M.G. Coy Appendix No. 4 October 1917		
Miscellaneous	213th Machine Gun Company Training Programme Oct 15th To Oct 20th 1917	20/10/1917	20/10/1917
Heading	213th M.G. Coy Appendix No.5 October 1917		
Miscellaneous	Company Routine Orders by Capt. L.A. Pollak Cmdg 213th M.G. Coy.	01/10/1917	01/10/1917
Miscellaneous	Company Routine Orders by Capt. L.A. Pollak Cmdg. 213th M.G. Coy.	07/10/1917	07/10/1917
Miscellaneous	Company Routine Orders by Capt. L.A. Pollak Cmdg. 213th M.G. Coy	15/10/1917	15/10/1917
Miscellaneous	Company Routine Orders by Capt. L.A. Pollak Cmdg. 213th M.G. Coy.	21/10/1917	21/10/1917
Heading	213th M.G. Coy Appendix No.6 October 1917		
Operation(al) Order(s)	213th Machine Gun Company Daily Order Part II No.1	10/10/1917	10/10/1917
Operation(al) Order(s)	213th Machine Gun Company Daily Orders Part 2 No. 2	17/10/1917	17/10/1917
Operation(al) Order(s)	213th Machine Gun Company Daily Orders Part II No. 3	24/10/1917	24/10/1917
Operation(al) Order(s)	213th Machine Gun Company Daily Order Part II No 4		
Heading	213th M.G. Coy. Appendix No 7 October 1917		
Miscellaneous	Company Orders by Capt. L.A. Pollak Cmdg. 213th M.G. Coy	30/10/1917	30/10/1917
Heading	213th M.G. Coy. Appendix No7 Oct 1917		
Heading	War Diary of 213th Machine Gun Coy From 1/11/17 To 30/11/17 Volume No.9		
War Diary	Monchiet	01/11/1917	13/11/1917
War Diary	Achiet Le Petit	14/11/1917	16/11/1917
War Diary	Lechelle	17/11/1917	19/11/1917
War Diary	Havrincourt Wood	20/11/1917	20/11/1917
War Diary	Havrincourt	21/11/1917	23/11/1917
War Diary	Bertincourt	24/11/1917	25/11/1917
War Diary	F 14 C	26/11/1917	28/11/1917
War Diary	K.9.c.7.0.	29/11/1917	29/11/1917
War Diary	Lebucquiere	30/11/1917	30/11/1917
War Diary	K.9.c.7.0.	30/11/1917	30/11/1917
Heading	Appendix No.1 213th M.G. Coy. November 1917		
Operation(al) Order(s)	213th Machine Gun Company Operation Order No. 14	13/11/1917	13/11/1917
Heading	Appendix No.2 213th M.G. Coy. November 1917		
Miscellaneous	To All Officers	10/11/1917	10/11/1917
Miscellaneous	Preliminary Instructions No.1	10/11/1917	10/11/1917
Heading	Appendix No.3 213th M.G. Coy. November 1917		
Miscellaneous	213th Machine Gun Company Preliminary Scheme	16/11/1917	16/11/1917
Miscellaneous	213th Machine Gun Coy Amendment To Preliminary Scheme	16/11/1917	16/11/1917
Miscellaneous	Addenda to Preliminary Scheme	18/11/1917	18/11/1917
Miscellaneous	213th Machine Gun Company Preliminary Instructions 2	17/11/1917	17/11/1917
Miscellaneous	Addenda to Preliminary Instructions No.2	17/11/1917	17/11/1917
Operation(al) Order(s)	213th Machine Gun Company Daily Orders Part II No. 8	29/11/1917	29/11/1917
Heading	Appendix No.4 213th M.G. Coy November 1917		
Miscellaneous	Company Routine Orders by Capt. L.A. Pollak Cmdg. 213th M.G. Coy.	02/09/1917	02/09/1917
Miscellaneous	Company Routine Orders by Capt. L.A. Pollak Cmdg. 213th M.G. Coy.	04/11/1917	04/11/1917

Miscellaneous	Company Routine Orders by Capt. L.A. Pollak Cmdg. 213th M.G. Coy.	07/11/1917	07/11/1917
Operation(al) Order(s)	213th Machine Gun Company Daily Orders Part II No. 8	22/11/1917	22/11/1917
Heading	Appendix No.5 213th M.G. Coy November 1917		
Miscellaneous	No. 7 (page 2)		
Operation(al) Order(s)	213th Machine Gun Company Daily Orders Part II No. 6	15/11/1917	15/11/1917
Operation(al) Order(s)	213th Machine Gun Company Daily Orders Part II No. 5	07/11/1917	07/11/1917
Heading	War Diary of 213th Machine Gun Coy From 1/12/17 To 31/12/17 (Volume 10)		
War Diary	Lock No. 7 Canal Du Lord	01/12/1917	03/12/1917
War Diary	Labuciere	04/12/1917	04/12/1917
War Diary	Bellacourt	05/12/1917	05/12/1917
War Diary	Habarcq	06/12/1917	06/12/1917
War Diary	Tincquette	07/12/1917	10/12/1917
War Diary	Vendin	11/12/1917	14/12/1917
War Diary	Lehamel	15/12/1917	18/12/1917
War Diary	Vendin	19/12/1917	19/12/1917
War Diary	Tincquette	20/12/1917	31/12/1917
Heading	Appendix I 213 M.G. Coy December 1917		
Operation(al) Order(s)	213th Machine Gun Company Operation Order No. 15	09/12/1917	09/12/1917
Heading	Appendix II 213 M.G. Coy. December 1917		
Operation(al) Order(s)	213th Machine Gun Company Operation Order No. 16	13/12/1917	13/12/1917
Heading	Appendix III 213 M.G. Coy. December 1917		
Operation(al) Order(s)	213th Machine Gun Company Daily Orders Part II No. 9	07/12/1917	07/12/1917
Operation(al) Order(s)	213th Machine Gun Company Daily Orders Part II No. 10	13/12/1917	13/12/1917
Operation(al) Order(s)	213th Machine Gun Company Daily Orders Part II No. 11	20/12/1917	20/12/1917
Operation(al) Order(s)	213th Machine Gun Company Daily Orders Part II No. 12	27/12/1917	27/12/1917
Heading	Appendix IV 213 M.G. Coy December 1917		
Miscellaneous	Company Routine Orders by Capt. L.A. Pollak Cmdg. 213th M.G. Coy.	29/12/1917	29/12/1917
Heading	War Diary of 213th Machine Gun Coy. From January 1st 1918 To January 31st 1918 Volume 11		
War Diary	Tincquette	01/01/1918	14/01/1918
War Diary	Anzin	15/01/1918	15/01/1918
War Diary	Coy H.Q. M. Railway Cutting Near Bailleul	16/01/1918	23/01/1918
War Diary	Anzin	24/01/1918	31/01/1918
Heading	Appendix I 213th M.G. Coy. Jany 1918		
Operation(al) Order(s)	213th Machine Gun Company Operation Order No.17	08/01/1918	08/01/1918
Operation(al) Order(s)	213th Machine Gun Company Operation Order No.18	13/01/1918	13/01/1918
Miscellaneous	Table Of Relief		
Miscellaneous	213th Machine Gun Company Amendment To O.O. No.18	14/01/1918	14/01/1918
Operation(al) Order(s)	213th Machine Gun Company Operation Order No. 19	21/01/1918	21/01/1918
Heading	Appendix II 213th M.G. Coy. January 1918		
Miscellaneous	213th Machine Gun Company Administrative Instruction	14/01/1918	14/01/1918
Heading	Appendix III 213th M.G. Coy. January 1918		
Miscellaneous	To All Officers	13/01/1918	13/01/1918
Heading	Appendix IIII 213th M.G. Coy. January 1918		

wps/2021/287(A)

wps/2021/287(T)

Vol XVIII

Army Form C. 2118.
ORIGINAL

WAR DIARY
or
~~INTELLIGENCE SUMMARY.~~
(Erase heading not required.)

2/4 Hampshire Regiment

Place	Date	Hour	Summary of Events and Information	Remarks and references to Appendices
	Nov. 1st		The Battalion remained in billets at SOLESMES.	Ref. Map. Sheet 51 S.W. 1/20,000
	2nd		The Battalion moved via ROMERIES to ESCARMAIN and spent the night in billets there.	Rpt
	3rd	2330 hrs.	The Battalion left ESCARMAIN at 2330 hrs.	Rpt Sheet 51 A. SE 1/20000
	3rd-11th.		For dates from 3rd – 11th November (both inclusive) see Appendix I. (Narrative of Operations)	Appendix I. Narrative of Operations 3rd–11th Nov. 1918.
	11th	1100 hrs	Cessation of Hostilities.	Rpt
	12th-18th		The Battalion remained in billets in ST. LAZARE Area until the morning of the 18th.	Rpt
	18th	0830 hrs.	The Battalion moved by march route to COUSOLRE on the first stage of the march to GERMANY.	Rpt Ref Map. NAMUR. 8. 1/100,000.
	19th		The Battalion moved by march route to RAGNIES. [BELGIUM] crossing the Franco-Belgian frontier 2 kilom. NE of BOUSIGNIES at 1100 hrs.	Rpt
	20th		The Battalion moved by march route to TARCIENNE, and remained in billets there till 24th.	Rpt
	24th		The Battalion moved by march route to DEVANT-LES-BOIS, 3 kilom. NE of BIESME.	Rpt

62ND DIVISION
186TH INFY BDE

213TH MACHINE GUN COY.

MAR 1917-FEB 1918

62/166

Vol 1.

War Diary

213 Machine Gun Co'y.
186th Inf. Bde.

From March 1. 1917
To March 31. 1917
inclusive

Mar 17
—
Feb 18

Army Form C. 2118.

WAR DIARY
or
INTELLIGENCE SUMMARY.

(Erase heading not required.)

Instructions regarding War Diaries and Intelligence Summaries are contained in F. S. Regs., Part II. and the Staff Manual respectively. Title pages will be prepared in manuscript.

Place	Date	Hour	Summary of Events and Information	Remarks and references to Appendices
DEEPCUT	1/3/17	10.50 AM	Entrained for SOUTHAMPTON.	
SOUTHAMPTON	1/3/17	12.45 PM	Arrived SOUTHAMPTON.	
		3.30 PM	Personnel embarked on H.M.T. LONDONDERRY.	
			Animals embarked on H.M.T. VOLUMNIA	
			Vehicles remained behind & loaded following day on H.M.T. HUNSGROVE	
		7 PM	H.M.T. LONDONDERRY & H.M.T. VOLUMNIA sailed from SOUTHAMPTON. Personnel & animals.	
HAVRE	2/3/17	7.30 AM	Disembarked at HAVRE & proceeded to No 2 REST CAMP	
	3/3/17	8.45 AM	Transport (Vehicles) arrived, unloaded & hauled to No 2. REST CAMP	
	4/3/17		At No 2. REST CAMP 1. O.R. To HOSPITAL	
	5/3/17			
	7/3/17	3 PM	Company left No 2. REST CAMP & entrained at PONT No 3	
		6.30 PM		
		9.30 PM	LEFT HAVRE	
ACHEUX	8/3/17	9.30 PM	DETRAINED AT ACHEUX	
		12 PM	Left ACHEUX & marched to ENGLEBELMER. Roads very bad making transport difficult	
ENGLEBELMER	9/3/17	2 AM	Arrival at ENGLEBELMER & billeted at BELTONPARK CAMP.	
			Company finally settled at 4 AM	

Army Form C. 2118.

WAR DIARY
or
INTELLIGENCE SUMMARY.
(Erase heading not required.)

Place	Date	Hour	Summary of Events and Information	Remarks and references to Appendices
ENGLEBELMER	9/3/17	7.30 pm	CAPT COLLYER reported to 62nd D.H.Q. & was informed that 213 Company was attached to 186th INFANTRY BRIGADE other Companies in Division were Nos 32, 34, 208, & also 212, which Easter had around with this company	
"	10/3/17	3 pm	Inspected by BRIGADIER GENERAL HILL Commanding 186th INFANTRY BRIGADE who was extremely pleased with the turnout	
"	11/3/17	10.15 am	Inspected by MAJOR GENERAL W.P. BRAITHWAITE C.B. Commanding 62nd DIVISION Splendid turnout MAJOR GENERAL W.P. BRAITHWAITE C.B. absolutely satisfied	
"	12/3/17		SGT CAMPBELL and SGT SOMERSET to HOSPITAL	
"	13/3/17		Received orders to prepare two complete sections for line	
"	14/3/17	11.30 AM	No. 2 & 4 sections proceeded to line attached to No 208 M.G. Coy. No 4 section actuated at Beaumont BEAUCOURT & No 2 section at L32 R32	
"	15/3/17	11.30 AM	No 1 Section moved up to BEAUCOURT. No 4 section two proceeded to MIRAU-MONT Brickfields the from of this section on employment in GUDGEON TRENCH	
"	16/3/17	10.00 AM	Received orders from 3H Inf Bde to employ & guns attached at gun pits near GUDGEON TRENCH to form a barrage on the 15K mtr on an attack by 186 BDE. on ACHIET LE PETIT. C.O. and O.i.c. No 4 section reconnoitred R. ground. Coy H.Q. moved from ET BALTON PARK to ENGLEBELMER. No 3 section moved to BEAUCOURT.	
"	17/3/17	10.00 AM	No.1 section moved from BEAUCOURT to MIRAUMONT Brickfields. No.4 section moved from MIRAUMONT to G.26 a 6.9 (ref 57D N.E.4) as the Germans have evacuated ACHIET LE PETIT and ACHIET LE GRAND	

Army Form C. 2118.

WAR DIARY
or
INTELLIGENCE SUMMARY.
(Erase heading not required.)

Instructions regarding War Diaries and Intelligence Summaries are contained in F. S. Regs., Part II. and the Staff Manual respectively. Title pages will be prepared in manuscript.

Place	Date	Hour	Summary of Events and Information	Remarks and references to Appendices
ENGLEBELMER	18.3.17	9.00 AM	Coy HQ moved from ENGLEBELMER to MIRAUMONT Briquetries. Coy intend to form part of advance guard (at 6.00 am) cancelled at 3.00 P.M. No1 Section proceeded to position north of ACHIET LE PETIT.	
MIRAUMONT	19.3.17	9.00 AM	Remained in positions. Tartare up on 18th inst.	
" "	20.3.17	9.00 AM	No change in position. Btn. H.Q. moved to ACHIET LE PETIT.	
" "	21.3.17	9.00 PM	No change in position.	
" "	22.3.17	9.30 PM	2Lt CROSSE proc to a/s courses at FORCEVILLE. No change in position	
ACHIET LE GD.	23.3.17	10.00 PM	Coy HQ and No's 2+4 Sections move into billets in ACHIET LE GRAND.	
" "	24.3.17	9.00 PM	Nos 1+3 Sections return coy in billets.	
" "	25.3.17	10.00 AM	OC reconnoitred the German trench system ERVILLERS - BEHAGNIES with G.O.C. 62nd DIVN and G.S.O.1 62nd DIVN. and intend to prepare a machine gun defence scheme on this line.	SEE APPENDIX 1.
" "	26.3.17	9.00 AM	Coy employed under R.E. on work on the above line. No 4 section moved to Pt B central (ref 57C) occupying as billets some old German dugouts and remains of shelters at EPINS to hospital with pyrexia. Coy HQ moved to Pt B central (ref 57C). Lt CROSSE returned from his course	
Pt B central (57C)	27.3.17	10. AM		
" "	28.3.17	10. AM	Coy still employed digging and wiring line.	
" "	29.3.17	10. PM	No change in position. Coy employed as yesterday.	
" "	30.3.17	10. PM	do	
" "	31.3.17	10. PM	do	

C.W. Cowper Maj
O.C. 213 M.G. Coy

APPENDIX I. R.F. 1/20000   Machine Gun Positions on the 62nd Divisional Front

SECRET.

Original

Confidential

War Diary

of

213 Coy M.G.C

From 1st April 1917 to 30th April 1917

Volume 2

Vol 2

Army Form C. 2118.

WAR DIARY
or
INTELLIGENCE SUMMARY.
(Erase heading not required.)

Instructions regarding War Diaries and Intelligence
Summaries are contained in F. S. Regs., Part II.
and the Staff Manual respectively. Title pages
will be prepared in manuscript.

Place	Date	Hour	Summary of Events and Information	Remarks and references to Appendices
G.b. † central ref 57C	1/4/17	8.30 AM	Company employed wiring and digging emplacements on the defensive line ERVILLERS - BEHAGNIES.	Bat
"	2/4/17	2.PM	Transport employed moving grenades from MIRAUMONT to SAPIGNIES.	Bat
"	3/4/17	8.30 AM	No change in position. Company employed as y'day.	Bat
"	"	8.30 AM	Company employed as on previous days.	Bat
"	"	12. Noon	3 shells from H.V. guns, apparently fired from some point S.W. of our position, fell within 500 yards of us, in the open fields	Bat
"	4/4/17	8.30 AM	Company employed as on previous days. 2.Lt GULSTON sent on A.A course at FIENVILLERS	Bat
"	5/4/17	8.30 AM	Company employed as on previous days. In addition to other fatigues, transport ordered to move wire from ACHIET LE GRAND to ERVILLERS. OC. Coy appointed D.M.G.O.	Bat
"	6/4/17	8.30 AM	Company employed as on previous days	Bat
"	7/4/17	8.30 AM	Four sections with fighting limbers and guns moved to MORY. Coy H.Q. and Transport to move tomorrow	Bat
"	8/4/17	9.30 AM	Company (at MORY) placed at disposal of CRE for work on roads. Transport employed hauling R.E material from CRE dump at ACHIET LE GRAND. This holds up own move and Coy HQ and signals remain this location. O/C with M.G.O. 5th Corps reconnoitre SECOND Cruz. Coy HQ moved to MORY	Bat
MORY	9/4/17	8.30 AM	1 and R Section work on defensive line - VAULX VRACOURT to L'HOMME MORT. 3 and 4 Sections work by night. At 4.P.M ordered to be ready to move on 10 mins notice. Transport moved up to MORY.	Bat
"	10/4/17	12.30 AM	Ordered to be ready to move at 5.00 AM	
"	"	5.15 "	Ordered to send 15 limbers to draw petrol for 2nd/4th at 4.00 AM. This carried out during course of the morning	
"	"	2.30 P.M	Orders for move cancelled. 1 + 2 Sections resume work on line	
"	"		Recd. order to take up position on 2nd line of defence with 208 M.G.Coy on left, 213 M.G.Coy on right at 27th Divn Down reported at BOIS E COURT but attack not expected. No.3 section to hold + guns on this line. No 4 section + guns in support. Transport with 1 and 2 sections move to B27C -	Bat
"	11/4/17	9.30 P.M	Coy ordered to concentrate at MORY and be ready to move in to wait AB at 6.00 AM on 11th inst	
"	"	6.0 AM	Coy ready to move	
"	"	10.0 "	No1 section RHA 21 D.T.W + ordered to advance to E COURT but were recalled at 11.00 AM as ANZAC Corps on our right attacked and held HINDENBURG LINE from 4.30 AM to 12.00 N. Rest were driven out	Bat
"	12/4/17	10.30 AM	Ordered to send 3 sections into front line to relieve 212 M.G.Coy. 208 M.G.Coy took over left sector held some long bridges to be ready to form an advance guard. L. TEARING returns from hospital	Bat

WAR DIARY
or
INTELLIGENCE SUMMARY.

Army Form C. 2118.

(Erase heading not required.)

Instructions regarding War Diaries and Intelligence Summaries are contained in F. S. Regs., Part II and the Staff Manual respectively. Title pages will be prepared in manuscript.

Place	Date	Hour	Summary of Events and Information	Remarks and references to Appendices
MORY	13/4/17	8:20 AM	Company remained disposed as yesterday. One O.R. slightly wounded by shell fire	Ref
"	14/4/17	8:20 AM	No change. One O.R. wounded	Ref
"	15/4/17	8:00 AM	2/LT. GUISTON returned from M.A. course. Section in reserve (Brit) stood to. Anxious to take up 2nd line as the enemy raided LAGNICOURT on our right. Artillery activity noticeable on our front all day. Booklets as issued were kept to be used. Three O.R. wounded.	
"	16/4/17	8:00 AM	by prisoners that gun would be used. Three O.R. wounded. Transport employed drawing iron and wire from 9:5 essential. No change in disposition of Coy.	Ref
"	"	8:15 PM	No's 3 and 4 Sections relieved No's 1 and 2 in front line. Enemy shelled this locality with H.E. about midnight. No damage done	
"	17/4/17 12 N.		Unusual artillery activity noticeable from 10:0 am. continued during day. No change in disposition of Coy.	Ref
"	19/4/17	11:02 AM	Transport again employed by R.E. Sections 3 and Transport lines shelled with H.E. No casualties to personnel but some saddlery and material destroyed and 4 horse wounded. Other units on same ground had several casualties. On 19th Coy moved to	Ref
B28 a 00			B28 a 00 (ref 57 c N.W.) 2 O.R. admitted hospital – still sick.	
"	19/4/17	8:30 AM	No change in disposition of Gun and Teams) relieved by 91st M.G. Coy. 1 O.R. WOUNDED.	Ref
"		10:00 PM	Sections 3 and 4 (less one gun and Team) relieved by 91st M.G. Coy.	
"	20/4/17	8:20 AM	No change in disposition of Coy. Coy Commander attached to 62nd Divn H.Q. as D.M.G.O. LT. R.N. EKINS assumes command of Coy with LT. R.H. JOYCE as 2nd in C.	Ref
"	21/4/17	4:20 AM	Coy employed cleaning guns and equipment – making shelter it	
"	22/4/17	8:20 AM	Coy attended Church Parade.	Ref
"	23/4/17	11:30 AM	ON HINDENBURG LINE Section officers made a reconnaissance of the ground over which the attack will be practised. No 4 Section only took part (with pack mules) in the practise of the attack. Remainder of Coy carried out Daily training as per programme	Ref
"	24/4/17	9 AM	Coy carried out Daily training. The one gun + team which has remained in the line came out.	Ref
"	25/4/17	8 AM	Coy carried out Daily training programme.	Ref
"	26/4/17	8 AM	Coy carried out Daily training programme.	Ref
"	27/4/17	8 AM	Coy carried out Daily training programme.	Ref
"	28/4/17	8 AM	Coy carried out Daily training programme. LT McFARLANE and 1 O.R. sent to CAMIERS on M.G. course.	Ref
"	"	6 PM	No 2 Section relieved at night and 212 M.G. Coy in Second line.	Ref

Army Form C. 2118.

WAR DIARY
or
INTELLIGENCE SUMMARY

(Erase heading not required.)

Instructions regarding War Diaries and Intelligence Summaries are contained in F. S. Regs., Part II. and the Staff Manual respectively. Title pages will be prepared in manuscript.

Place	Date	Hour	Summary of Events and Information	Remarks and references to Appendices
B28 a 00	29/4/17	8. A.M	Coy carried out daily training programme. Instruction in German machine gun was given to machine gunners of Inf. Bde. in this Bde., two Coy having a German gun for the purpose	M9.
		9.30 p.m	Coy ordered to put itself in readiness to move on 10 minutes notice	
"	30/4/17	10.00 p.m	Coy ordered to put itself in readiness to move on 30 minutes notice and to carry on training	

Rbt. Joyce Lt
for OC. 213 M.G. Coy.

Original

Vol 3

Confidential
War Diary
of
213th Machine Gun Company

From 1st May 1917 to 31st May 1917

Volume 3

Army Form C. 2118.

213th Machine Gun Company

WAR DIARY
or
INTELLIGENCE SUMMARY
(Erase heading not required.)

Instructions regarding War Diaries and Intelligence Summaries are contained in F. S. Regs., Part II. and the Staff Manual respectively. Title pages will be prepared in manuscript.

Place	Date	Hour	Summary of Events and Information	Remarks and references to Appendices
B28.a.00 (57cNW)	1/5/17	7:00 AM	Today being "X" day the orders for the attack on the HINDENBERG LINE, the Coy was disposed as follows No1 Section in Embankment at ECOUST (U27C reference APPENDIX 1) Nos 2,3, and 4 Sections in 2ND LINE near B17.b.04 (Ref 57cNW 1/20,000) These moves completed by 10.PM	APP. NO.1 RHJ
"	2/5/17	8:00 AM	Position unchanged. Today "Y" day.	RHJ
"	3/5/17	7:00 PM	No1 Section already in Battle Positions. Nos 2,3,+ 4 Sections prepare to move into Battle positions.	RHJ
"	3/5/17	12:25 AM	Nos 2,3,+ 4 sections move into positions they will occupy at Zero hour according to operation order by Lt. R.N.EKINS. (Operation order and amendments APPENDIX 2). Coy HQ moved to B17.a.8.8 (Ref 57cNW 1/20,000)	APP. NO.2 RHJ
"	"	3:30 AM	All four sections in position according to operation order.	APP. NO.2
"	"	3:45 AM	Zero hour.	
"	"	1:00 AM	Reports at this time showed that the situation was not developing well as anticipated. The action taken by the Coy during the rest of the day is attached here (APPENDIX 3) Casualties APP. No 3	RHJ
"	4/5/17	7:00 PM	No 4 Section relieved in front line, by a composite section under 2Lt. GULSTON.	RHJ
"	5/5/17	8:00 AM	Coy remained disposed as yesterday	RHJ
"	6/5/17	7:00 PM	Composite section in front line was relieved by a section under 2Lt. DENT.	RHJ
"	"	11:00 PM	Orders recd to withdraw all guns of this Coy from front line.	RHJ
"	7/5/17	3:00 AM	All guns now withdrawn from front line.	
"	"	4:00 PM	Orders to relieve 201 M.G.Coy in left sector ie U25.C.52 to T29.a.98 with 12 guns (ref 51B S.W. 1/20,000) in vicinity of CROISELLES	RHJ
"	8/5/17	2:00 AM	Above relief complete.	RHJ
"	"	6:30 PM	Received reinforcement (9 NCOs + N.C.O) from CAMIERS	RHJ
"	9/5/17	9:00 AM	Received reinforcement (6 ORs, 2 NCOs) from CAMIERS. No change in disposition of company	RHJ
"	10/5/17	9:00 AM	No change in disposition of company	RHJ
"	11/5/17	9:00 AM	No change in disposition of company	RHJ
"	12/5/17	4:00 AM	6 guns in line laid a barrage on German Communication Trenches covering operations by the Division on our right - 37000 rounds fired.	RHJ
"	"	9:00 AM	No change in disposition of company. CPL COUSINS shot in Ankle. Two Horses at ACHIET LE PETIT	RHJ
"	13/5/17	9:00 AM	No change in disposition of company	RHJ

Army Form C. 2118.

23rd Machine Gun Company

WAR DIARY or INTELLIGENCE SUMMARY

(Erase heading not required.)

Place	Date	Hour	Summary of Events and Information	Remarks and references to Appendices
B28 a00 (57c NW)	14/5/17	3 P.M.	COY. H.Q. moved to B7 c 7.2. (57c NW) in accordance with BDE orders.	Ref.
B7 c 7.2 (57c NW)	15/5/17	2:30 P.M.	Ordered by DIVISION to move to vicinity of MORY COPSE, to occupy the 2ND DEFENSIVE LINE on relief from front line by 201 M.G. Coy. and to place all available men at disposal of R.E. at 9 A.M. 15TH inst.	Ref.
"	16/5/17	3:30 A.M.	The Coy. underwent the relief first. Relief complete- COY now has 12 guns on 2ND DEFENSIVE LINE from B4 d. 55 to B17 c Central (57c NW)	Ref.
"		3:30 P.M.	COY H.Q. moved to B15 & 23 (57c NW)	Ref.
		5:30 P.M.	Working party of 35 placed at disposal of R.E. for work on 2ND DEFENSIVE LINE	Ref.
B15 b 23 (57c NW)	17/5/17	9:30 A.M.	Coy. now disposed as follows:- No.'s 2,3 and 4 sections in 2ND DEFENSIVE LINE — No 1 Section, COY HQ and Transport Lines at B15 b 23. All available men at disposal of R.E. for work during course. CPL COUSINS returned from course.	Ref.
"	18/5/17	9:30 A.M.	Coy. remained disposed as yesterday — SGT. HAND sent on M.G. course to CAMIERS.	Ref.
"	19/5/17	9:30 A.M.	No change in disposition of Company.	Ref.
A16 c 68 (57c NW)	20/5/17	8:30 P.M.	Coy. H.Q. moved to A16 c 68 (57c NW) near COURCELLES 2,3 & 4 sections relieved from 2ND DEFENSIVE LINE and joined Company at new location. Lt. McFARLANE and SGT. CAMPBELL returned from course	Ref. Ref.
"	21/5/17	9 A.M.	Daily programme of work and training began.	Ref.
"	22/5/17	9 A.M.	Daily training programme carried out and list of deficiencies commenced.	Ref.
"	23/5/17	9 A.M.	Daily training programme carried out. It is noted that this is the first period of rest the Company as a whole has had since first week in March.	Ref.
"	24/5/17	9 A.M.	Daily training programme carried on. Visited by BRIG-GEN. HILL.	Ref.
"	25/5/17	9 A.M.	Inspected by M.G.O. V Corps.	Ref.
"		2 P.M.	Daily training programme continued. LT. EKINS sent on leave.	Ref.
"	26/5/17	9 A.M.	Daily training programme continued.	Ref.
"	27/5/17	11 A.M.	Coy attended church parade.	Ref.
"		2 A.M.	Received orders to occupy the 2ND DEFENSIVE LINE from B2L d 67. to L'HOMME MORT mill near of 57c NW.	Ref.

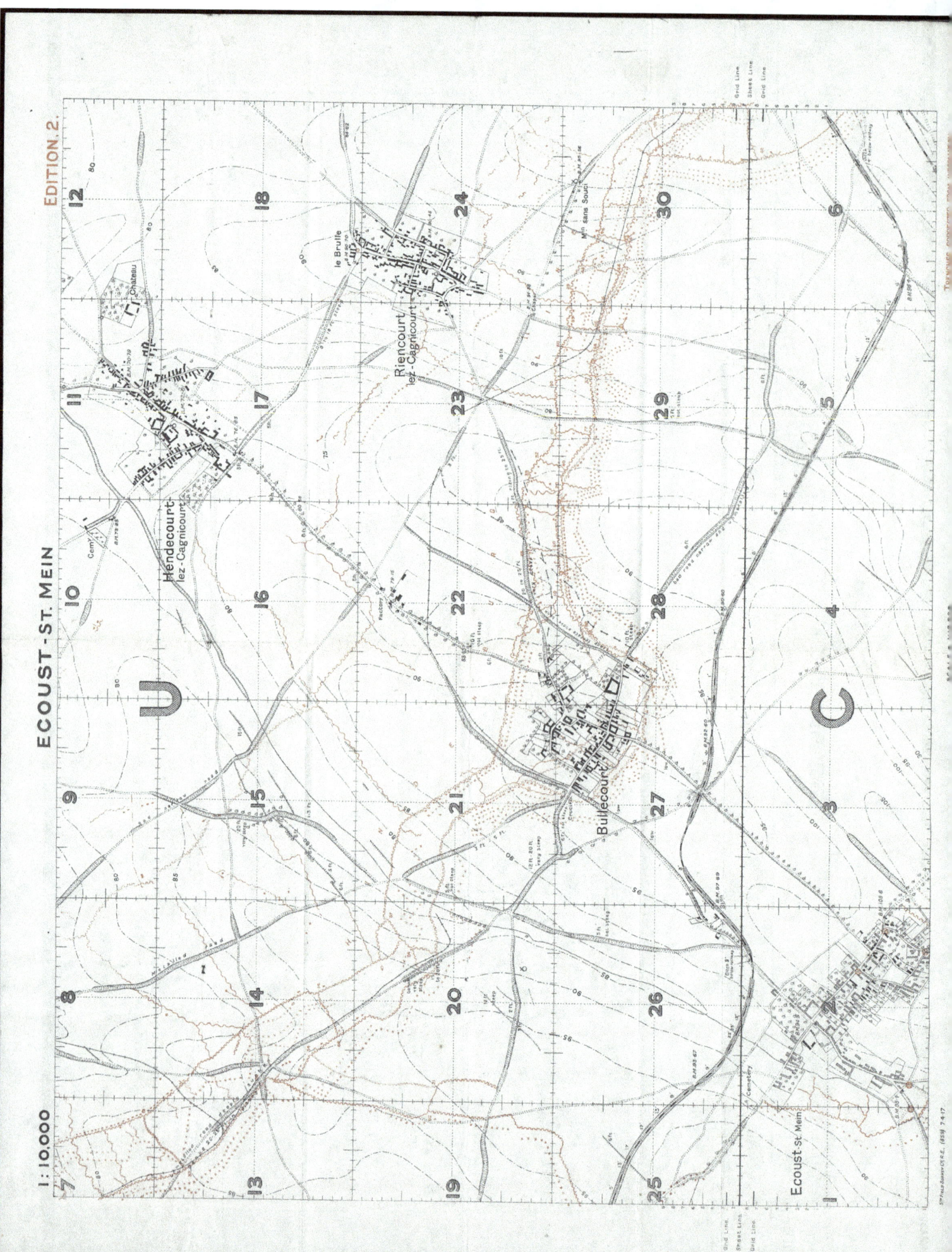

Original

Confidential
Appendix No. 1
War Diary 213 M.I. Coy.
Map ECOUST. ST. MEIN 1/10.000

Army Form C. 2118.

WAR DIARY
or
INTELLIGENCE SUMMARY. 213 Machine Gun Company
(Erase heading not required.)

Instructions regarding War Diaries and Intelligence Summaries are contained in F. S. Regs., Part II. and the Staff Manual respectively. Title pages will be prepared in manuscript.

Place	Date	Hour	Summary of Events and Information	Remarks and references to Appendices
A16 C.6.8 (57C NW)	28/5/17	9 AM	LT. R.H. JOYCE and 2LT. McFARLANE reported to O.C. Troops in 2nd line and made arrangements for relief of guns now there belonging to 58TH DIVN. Also arranged for Company to concentrate in vicinity of MORY and site for Camp was selected at B.27 d.1.8. Orders issued for relief.	Ref
"	29/5/17	8 AM	No 3 section and 2 guns No 2 Section proceeded to 2ND LINE. under 2LT McFARLANE.	
		9 AM	Advance party under LT CROSSE left for new camp.	
		1 PM	Company (less officers) billets which were turned over to 91ST. M.G. COY.	Ref
		4 PM	Company now in Camp at new location.	
B27 d.1.8 (57C NW)	30/5/17	9 AM	Working party (50) employed under R.E. for work in 2ND LINE. CAPT. H.O. COLLYER re-assumed his command of the Company on this date.	Ref
"	31/5/17	9 AM	No change in distribution or employment of Company	Ref

R.H. Joyce Lieut.
for O.C. 213 M.G. Coy

Original

Confidential

Appendix No 2

War Diary   213 MG Coy

Operation order and amendments
Attack on HINDENBURG LINE 3.5.17

COPY NO. 11

213 Machine Gun Coy. Operation Order No 1

B22 b 68
16.4.17

Reference
Maps 51B S.W., 57C N.W.

I. INFORMATION

The 62nd Divn will attack the HINDENBURG LINE between U20 b06 and U28 a41 on Z day (not before 18th inst.)

The boundaries of 186th Bde. will be as follows:—
LEFT BOUNDARY U26 c36 to U20 d94 to U21 a51 to U16 a00 to U10 b50.
RIGHT BOUNDARY The roadway U27 a67 to U27 b 1380 to U21 d36 to U22 b29.

187th Bde. will be on the left and 185th Bde on the right. The taped line for the Bde. will be from U27 a 82 to U20 d94.

The FIRST OBJECTIVE of the Divn will be the German trench U21 d32 to U20 a96 and the German trench from U22 c93 to U14 d30. The SECOND OBJECTIVE will be the line of roadway from U22 b85 to U16 c45 to German trench U15 d95 to U15 a85. The THIRD OBJECTIVE will be a line running from U12 c77 to U11 b80 to U9 d24 to U15 a56.

The 185th. Bde. will not advance beyond the first objective. The attack of the 186th Bde. will be carried out with 2/5 D. of W. REGT. on the right and 2/6 D. of W. on the left. The dividing line between the Bns. will be a line from U21 c41 to U21 b1505. The 2/4 D of W will take the SECOND OBJECTIVE and when the position has been consolidated it will be taken over by 2/4 BN. W. YORKS lent for the occasion and the 2/4 D of W. will enter advance on the THIRD OBJECTIVE.

After leaving the FIRST OBJECTIVE the 186th Bde. will gain touch with the SECOND AUSTRALIAN DIVN. who will attack on the right of the 185th Bde. The advance from the first to the second objective will commence at 0 + 75 mins and from the second to the third objective at 0 + 135 mins.

II. M.G. DISPOSITIONS, 213 COY.

No 1 SECTION will be in position at U27 c with two guns in the German dugout at U27 c 27 and two guns at U27 c 96 for the purpose of covering the 186th and 185th Bdes should the assault be unsuccessful. They will only fire in the event of the assault being unsuccessful, and must on no account disclose their positions. If the assault is successful these guns will remain in position and await orders.

Nos 2 and 3 SECTIONS will be in position under cover in the road in U26 b. Each section commander will send forward a N.C.O. to a position where he can observe the German trenches in U21 a, b, and d. When the Infy have taken the 2nd trench of the 1st. objective these sections will move forward and consolidate on the line of the 2nd trench.

No 2 SECTION will be on the right and two guns will be detailed to face BULLECOURT should the attack of the 185th Bde be held up. When BULLECOURT is captured these two guns will take up positions as required on the general alignment NORTH WEST of BULLECOURT. 2 GUNS No 3 SECTION will be on the left and will be prepared to push forward into advanced positions in U21 b to facilitate the advance on the 2nd objective.

When Nos 2 and 3 SECTIONS advance they will form an advanced dump of ammunition belts at U26 b.

No 4 SECTION will be in reserve at the RY. EMBANKMENT at U26 c52 with 4 pack mules, ready to move forward to the 2nd and 3rd OBJECTIVES on receipt of orders from O.C. COY.

III. PERSONNEL TAKING PART IN THE ATTACK

LT. R.N. EKINS will be in command of 213 M.G. COY as CAPT. H.O. COLLYER will be employed in his capacity as D.M.G.O. Following officers & N.C.O.S and men will remain in transport lines at L'ABBAYE MORT:— LT. R.H. JOYCE, C.Q.M.S., SGTS. HAND and FULFORD, CPLS TWIGG and ATTWOOD, storeman, three cooks, coy clerk, two waterman. Officers servants will accompany their masters, remaining men to be at advanced Coy H.Q.

IV. H.Q. and REPORT CENTRES

ADVANCED COY H.Q. will be in a dugout at about U25 d52 where all reports will be sent. H.Q. of units as follows, DIVN at ACHIET LE GRAND with report centre at B13 b23 — 185th Bde at B17 b24 — 186 and 187 Bdes at L'HOMME MORT — 2/4 2/5 2/6 D of W. at RY EMBANKMENT U26 c — 2/7 D of W at C2 d 88 — advanced 185th Bde HQ at B6 d 45. All ranks must be impressed of the necessity of sending back information.

V. DRESS

Fighting order, haversacks on back, water bottles carried then to be full at commencement of operations, box respirators to be worn in "alert" position, water proof sheets to be carried, great coats will not be worn. Each man will carry 2 iron rations which will not be eaten except on orders of OC. Coy. or in extreme emergency.

The guns going forward in the first instance will only carry auxiliary mountings the Mk IV tripod to be left at Coy H.Q. at U25 d52 and will be brought forward when the situation permits.

VI. AMMUNITION SUPPLY

Ammunition dump with B.F. machines will be at Coy H.Q. U25 d52, every effort must be made to send back empty belts to be filled.

Ronald N Ekins Lieut
CAPTAIN
O.C. 213 M.G. COY.

Amendment to
213 M.G. Coy.
Operation order No 1.

Copy No. 11.

21/4/17

Re: para 1. a/ For "The 2/4th D of W's Regt will take the 2nd objective – – – – – advance on the 3rd objective – substitute: –

"The 2/7th D of W's Regt. on the right & the"
"2/4th D of W's Regt. on the left will attack the 2nd"
"objective & when the position is consolidated, it"
"will be taken over by 3 Coys of the 2/8th West Yorks"
"Regt prior to O + 2 hours. The 2/7th & 2/4th D of W's"
"Regt will then advance on the 3rd objective"

b/ The dividing line between Battns will be a line from U 21.C 4.1. to U 21.b 15.05. thence to trench junction U 22.a.65.95. to junction of trench with road U 17a 20.35. to road junction U 17a 45.90. to road junction U 11 b 2.3. (All inclusive to the 2/7th D of W's Regt)

Re: para 2 a/ The 2 guns detailed from No 2 section to face Bullecourt will take up a position in the vicinity of U 21d 5.6.

b/ No 4 Section in reserve with pack mules will advance in conjunction with the 2/4th & 2/7th D of W's Regt against Hendecourt. When the final objective has been gained, guns will be located at the following strong points

(1) Factory — U 22 b 1.7. (2 guns)
(2) Roadway — U 17 a 8.0.
(3) Road junction — U 17.b. 3.6.

O/C No 4 Section will use his discretion as to how far the pack animals may be taken

Ronald Elkins Lieut
O/C 213 Coy
M.G.C.

Amendments & additions to 213 Coy M.G.C.   Copy No 11
Operation order No 1

1. Reference IV (a) Coy Hdqrs will be at L'HOMME MORT (B.17.a.8.7) Reports will be sent to Coy Runner Post stationed at the road junction at about U.26.d.55.00. From there they will be sent to Hdqrs via Battn Runner Post
(b) When Coy Hdqrs move forward, a notification will be sent to all concerned

2. (a) On X/Y night No 1 Section will relieve the 3 guns of the M.G Coy holding the line at {U.27.c.2.7 / U.26.c.5.2 / U.26.c.1.5}   No's 2.3.& 4. Sections will proceed to positions in the Second Line.
(b) On Y/Z night the coy will move into its battle positions as follows:—

Section	Time	Route	Pass Bde Dump at	Destination
2	12.15.A.M.	Along N side of MORY ECOUST	2.30.A.M.	U 26 d
3	12.18.A.M.	Rd B.17.b – B.12.c & b –	2.33.A.M.	U 26 d
4	12.20 A.M.	C.1.a & b to roadway S of cemetery at C.2.a.1.7 – C.2.b.1.9.	2.35 A.M.	U 26 c 7.0

(c) O/C No 1 Section will arrange to withdraw his guns from the Embankment & the one from C.8.b.2.0 into battle positions in U.27.c as soon as it is dark. Guns & teams from Embankment must be clear of Bde Dump at C.2.b.1.9. by 11.p.m.

3. (a) On Z day at 0+1 hour Lieut R.H. Joyce will report at Coy HDqrs with Pack Mules in readiness for the use of No 1 Section, & await orders.
(b) After the advance on the 3rd Objective. O.C. No 1 Section will on receipt of orders, load 4 guns & ammunition on to Pack Mules & proceed to HENDECOURT & will there distribute his guns in the following strong points:—
   a U.12.c.2.5 (2 guns)
   b U.11.b.1.2 (1 gun)
   c U.10.b.5.0 (1 gun)
These 4 guns together with the 2 guns of No 4 Section situated at U.17.a.8.0 & U.17.b.3.5. will form part of the garrison of HENDECOURT. under the command of Lt. Col. H.E.P.NASH o/c 2/4 D of W. Regt
(c) O's C No's 1 & 4 Sections will arrange to have their Hdqrs in the vicinity of U.17.a.1.7. adjacent to the Hdqrs of O.C. garrison
(d) The 2 guns at the FACTORY will be under the supervision of 2nd Lieut. D. MILLIKIN, who will also take over the 2 guns at {U.16.c.9.5 / U.16.c.9.0} from 2nd Lieut A.S. OULSTON. as soon as the situation permits

4. Watches will be synchronised at 12.15 p.m. & 6.15 p.m. on Y day

5. ALL MESSAGES AND REPORTS HOWEVER SENT MUST BEAR THE TIME, ADDRESS FROM, AND NAME OF SENDER.

6. Code names will not be used after Zero hour.

7. S.O.S. Signal will be green VERey LIGHTS or GREEN ROCKETS.

Ronald N Ekins Lieut:
o/c 213 Coy
M.G.C.

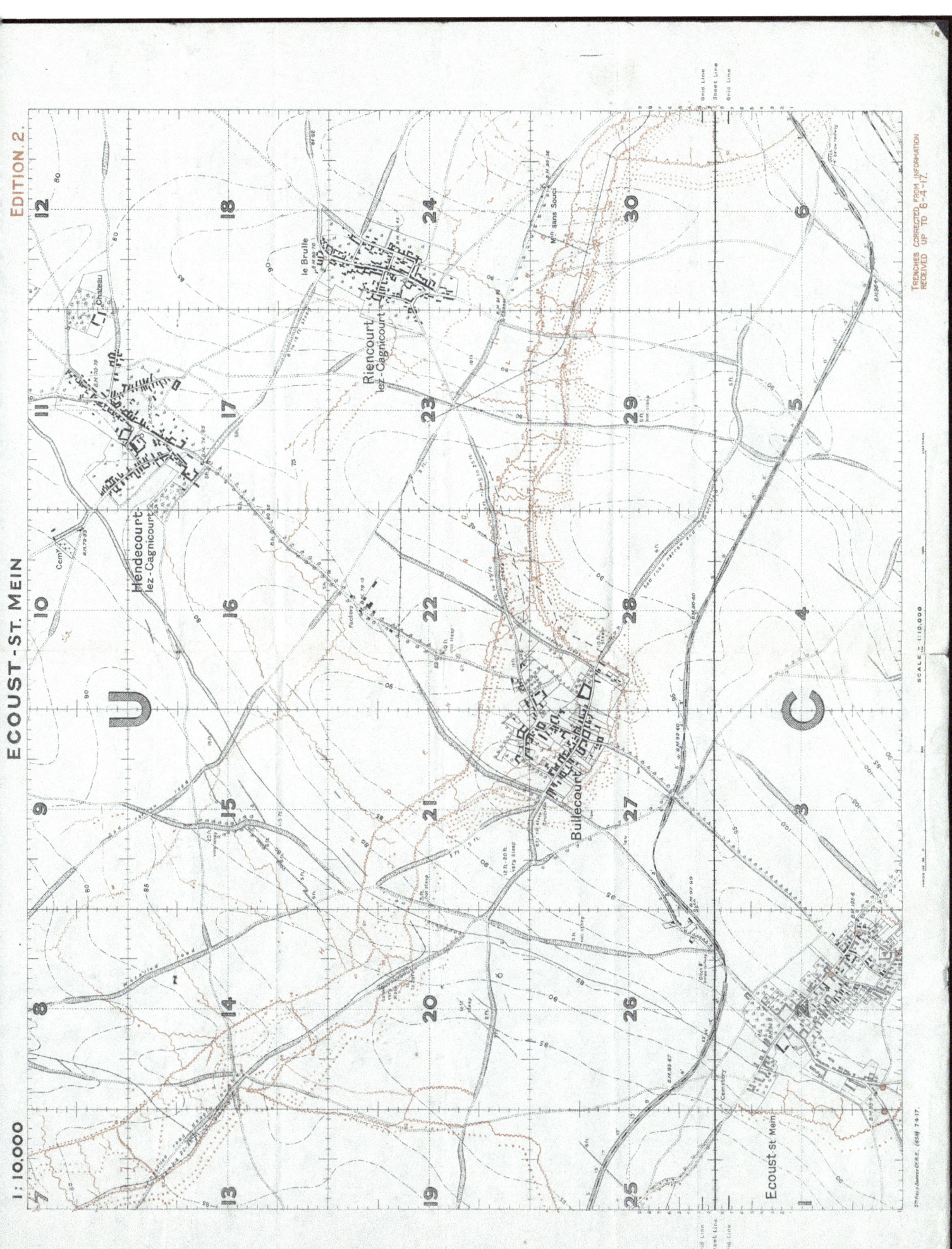

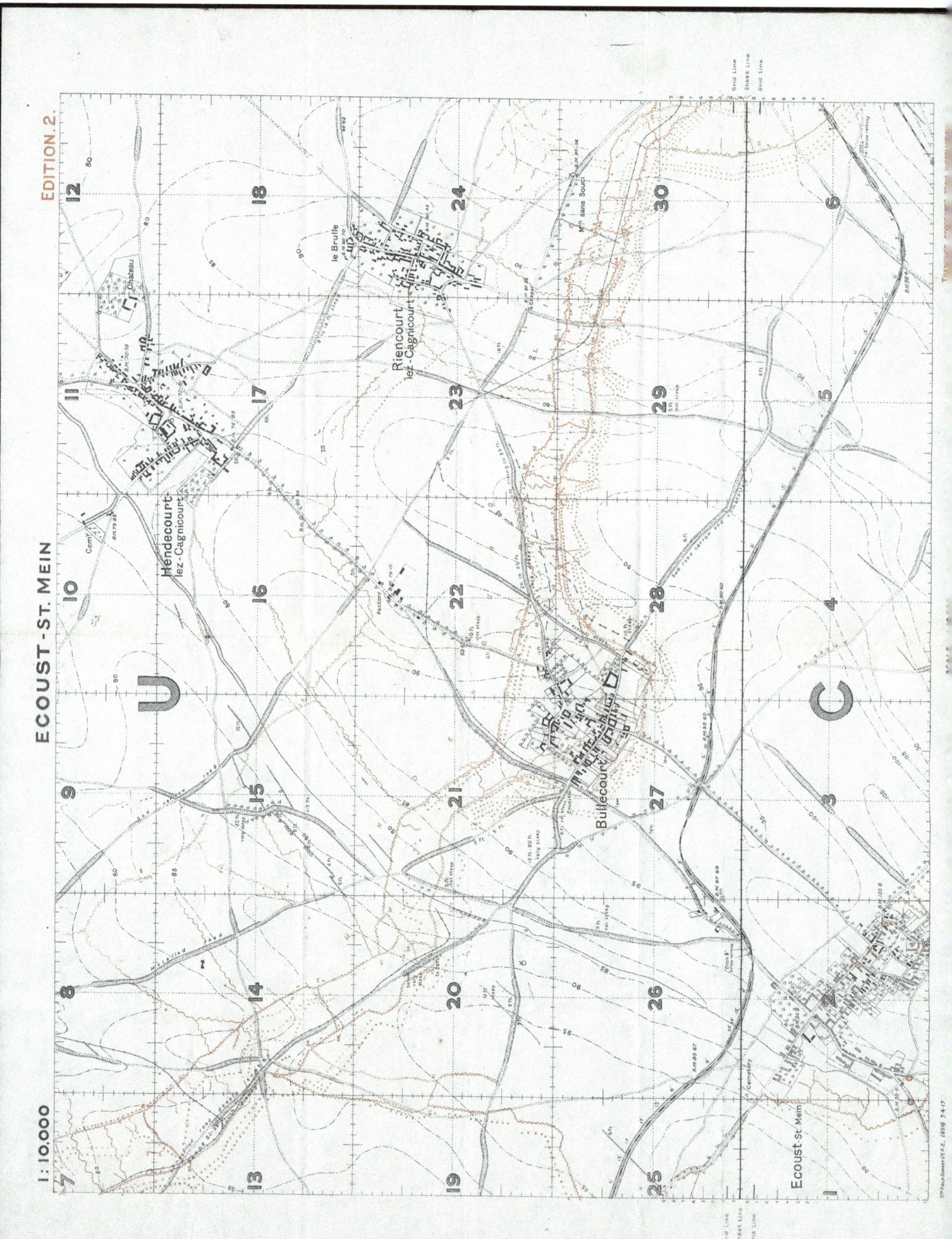

Original

Confidential
Appendix No. 1
War Diary 213 MG Coy
Map ECOUST - ST. MEIN 1/10.000

Original

Confidential
Appendix No. 1
War Diary 213 MG Coy
Map ECOUST-ST. MEIN 1/10.000

Original

Confidential
War Diary
of
213 Coy M.G.C.

Vol 4

From 1st June 1917 to 30th June 1917

Volumes 4

WAR DIARY or INTELLIGENCE SUMMARY

Army Form C. 2118.

213th Machine Gun Coy

(Erase heading not required.)

Place	Date	Hour	Summary of Events and Information	Remarks and references to Appendices
B28 G 4.5 (57c N.W)	1/6/17	9:00 AM	Coy H.Q. and transport lines moved to the location.*	Rmf
"	2/6/17	9:00 AM	No change in disposition of Coy. – daily training resumed	Rmf
"	3/6/17	9:00 AM	No change. Enemy shelled vicinity of MORY COPSE with gun of large calibre probably 12". 12 rounds fired about 4-5 P.M.	Rmf
"	4/6/17	9:00 AM	No change. Enemy shelled L'ABBAYE at MORY, and vicinity, with probably 5.9 howitzer. 15 rounds fired about 3-4 PM. Signal enemy planes seen thro' the day — all were out of M.G. range	Rmf
"	5/6/17	9:00 AM	No change. Enemy shelled trading S.W. of MORY and vicinity of our camp with small gun. Five to the afternoon and dropped upon near 2Lt SADDLETON relieved 2 and 3 sections in 2nd LINE. 1 and 4 sections bombed this area — no good observation of them could be had.	Rmf
"		5:00 P.M		Rmf
"	6/6/17	10:00 P.M	Enemy aircraft bombed this area — no good observation of them could be had.	Rmf
"	7/6/17	9:00 AM	No change. 2Lt GULSTON returned from leave	Rmf
"	8/6/17	9:00 AM	No change. *Lt EKINS returned from leave	Rmf
"	9/6/17	9:00 AM	No change.	Rmf
"	10/6/17	10 AM	Relieved from duty in 2nd line by 201 M.G. Coy and moved to ACHIET LE PETIT	Rmf
ACHIET LE PETIT	11/6/17	7 PM	Relief complete and Coy at ACHIET LE PETIT	Rmf
"	12/6/17	9 AM	Moved Camp 911 2m. off site because of mud. Cleaning guns and equipment	Rmf
"		10 PM	Adv. tactical scheme in progress. Practice alarm – Coy turned out in fighting order.	Rmf
"	13/6/17	9 AM	Moved camp to another site in village	Rmf
"	14/6/17	9 AM	Daily training programme commenced.	Rmf
"	15/6/17	9 AM	Daily training programme continued. Inspected by G.O.C. 62nd Divn	Rmf
"	16/6/17	9 AM	Daily training programme continued. CAPT. COLLYER went on leave	Rmf
"	17/6/17	10 AM	Church parade and service	Rmf
"	18/6/17	9 AM	Daily training programme continued	Rmf

WAR DIARY
or
INTELLIGENCE SUMMARY

(Erase heading not required.)

Army Form C. 2118.

213th Machine Gun Coy

Place	Date	Hour	Summary of Events and Information	Remarks and references to Appendices
GNET LE PETIT	19/6/17	9 A.M	Daily training programme continued	Ref
"	20/6/17	9 A.M	"	Ref
"	21/6/17	9 A.M	"	Ref
"	22/6/17	9 A.M	"	Ref
"	23/6/17	9 A.M	"	Ref
"	24/6/17	9 A.M	Sunday. Church Parade.	Ref
"	25/6/17	9 A.M	Cleaning guns and equipt. Preparing to proceed to line	Ref
"	26/6/17	9 A.M	Advance party under Lt. R.H.Joyce left for FAVREUIL area to take over Coy lines & camp etc.	
"		2.30 P.M	Coy moved off arriving at BEUGNATRE at 4.30 P.M (H18a. ref 57c N.W.) rested here. Temporary transport lines made here.	Ref
C16 & 12 N.W. (57c NW)	27/6/17	9.30 P.M 3.30 A.M	Coy started to move off to relieve 61 M.G Coy in front line NOREUIL SECTOR. Relief complete. Coy H.Q at C16 & 12 – 3 guns in line in U 29, 8 guns in C5, 5 guns in reserve at Coy HQs in NOREUIL SECTOR. Transport lines and Q.M. store at H18 a Central (57c N.W.)	
"	28/6/17	9 P.M	Capt H.D.COLLYER returned from leave and took command of Coy. Guns in line doing very little firing – nothing of interest to report. Work commenced immediately on trenches emplacements etc.	Ref Ref
"	29/6/17	9 A.M	No change in disposition of Coy – Lt EKINS proceeded to CAMIERS to attend course.	
"	30/6/17	9 A.M	No change in disposition of Coy.	
"		5.P.M	Capt COLLYER recalled to DIVN H.Q as Divnl M.G.O Lt R.H.JOYCE assumed command.	Ref.
"		10.P.M	5 guns at Coy H.Q laid on barrage lines in accordance with orders from Divn H.Q.	

R.H.Joyce Lieut.
M 213 M.G. Coy.

SECRET.

War Diary
of
2/3 Coy A.M.G.C.

Vol 5

From 1/7/17 to 31/7/17

Volume 5

WAR DIARY or INTELLIGENCE SUMMARY

Army Form C. 2118.

213th Machine Gun Company

Place	Date	Hour	Summary of Events and Information	Remarks and references to Appendices
16 G.12 (ref 57c N.W)	1/7/17	12.N.	Enemy Artillery and M.G.s very active during night and early morning.	Ref.
"		12.M.	Situation quiet. Work done on trench, emplacements and dug outs.	
"	2/7/17	12.N.	Enemy Artillery continued active thro' night. Enemy aircraft unusually active and two flying low over our positions in front line. Our guns fired using tracer bullets and hits were observed on 2 planes one being forced to descend near TRIENCOURT.	Ref.
"		12.M.	Situation quiet. Work continued.	Ref.
"	3/7/17	12.N.	Enemy Artillery active – firing on trenches no C.5.b.75.45 and C.5.b.77. 10 dug outs got two direct hits.	
"		12.M.	Enemy aircraft continue active – are being engaged by our M.G.s and the Inf. Lewis guns. Otherwise situation quiet. One casualty – accidental, two fully reports in APP.1.	Ref. APP.1.
"	4/7/17	12.N.	Situation quiet. Issued men for relief R.H.-1 in accordance with Bde Orders. Owing to the relieving Coy having only 9 guns available the relief will be incomplete.	Ref.
"		7.P.M.	Advance party 208 Coy came in.	
"		10.P.M.	Relief commenced.	
"	5/7/17	3.A.M.	Relief complete – except as noted in para. 1 section "b" of relief order.	
H.19.d (ref 57c N.W)		5.A.M.	Company in camp at marginally noted location.	Ref.
"		11.A.M.	Kit inspection and cleaning up generally – this took up most of the day.	
"	6/7/17	9.A.M.	A lot of work improving camp and wagon lines – cleaning limbers it was laid out and commenced. The whole day was given to this. 208 Coy completed relief.	Ref.
"	7/7/17	9.A.M.	Training Programme commenced and carried on. Lecture to N.C.O.s etc and indoor work done.	Ref.
"	8/7/17	9.A.M.	Heavy rain prevented out door work. Indoor work done.	Ref.
"	9/7/17	9.A.M.	Continued rain badly interferes with training – indoor work done. Inspected by Brig-Genl. Skill in afternoon.	Ref.

WAR DIARY
or
INTELLIGENCE SUMMARY

Army Form C. 2118.

213th Machine Gun Coy

(Erase heading not required.)

Place	Date	Hour	Summary of Events and Information	Remarks and references to Appendices
H18.d (57C NW)	10/7/17	9. AM	Daily training programme continued - one officer of two coy goes daily to look over the front line in the LAGNICOURT sector	Roof
— " —	11/7/17	9.30 AM	O.C. and N.C.O.'s made reconnaissance of front line returning to camp at noon. Coy continues daily training relieving some firing with bull running.	Roof
— " —	12/7/17	9. AM	Daily training continued	
		2. PM	Cleaning up and packing limbers - advance party under 2/Lt SADDLETON left for front line. Inspection of coy and billets by O.C.	
		6.30 PM	Coy started for front line to relieve 212 M.G.Coy according to orders No. R.H:2 See appendix no. II	APP I Roof
C22.d.8.0	13/7/17	12. AM	Relief complete. Situation very quiet.	Roof
— " —	14/7/17	12. N	Situation very quiet, no firing done except A.A. by guns detailed for this work.	Roof
— " —	15/7/17	12. N	Situation very quiet. Reconnoitred some positions for overhead fire	Roof
— " —	16/7/17	12. N	Situation quiet	
		12. M	Provided covering fire to assist in raid - see appendix III	APP III Roof
— " —	17/7/17	4 AM	Raid was unsuccessful, no firing was done. Two guns "stood to" for 3 hours in rain.	
		12. N	Situation quiet - battery positions in the locality shelled with 10.5 m. about noon.	Roof
— " —	18/7/17	12. N	Situation quiet. Weather for past 2 days dull and rainy.	Roof
		12. M	Carried out overhead fire from C17.b.72 - Target LAGNICOURT-QUEANT road enfiladed and Crucifix triangle in D.8.C. Fire unobserved but at these points movement is continually seen.	Roof
— " —	19/7/17	12. N	Enemy shelled this locality with 10.5 m. at 10.30 A.M. no casualties - several duds counted. O/C 2/6 D.L.W. asks that our overhead fire be stopped - causing his troops in front some annoyance. Our shots are passing 100 yds over their heads.	Roof

Army Form C. 2118.

WAR DIARY
or
INTELLIGENCE SUMMARY

(Erase heading not required.)

Army Form C. 2118.

213/Machine Gun Coy

Instructions regarding War Diaries and Intelligence Summaries are contained in F.S. Regs., Part II. and the Staff Manual respectively. Title pages will be prepared in manuscript.

Place	Date	Hour	Summary of Events and Information	Remarks and references to Appendices
C.22.d.80	20/7/17	12 M	Situation quiet – there was a sudden intense bombardment of our left sector from 1 PM to 1.10 PM – believed to be enemy T.M.'s firing on trenches in U.29.y. No 3 Section relieved No 2 Section in RIGHT SUB-SECTOR on night of 20/21ST. 2/LT. D. MILLIKIN returned from Course. Situation quiet all day.	Rep
"	21/7/17	12 N.		Rep
"	22/7/17	12 N.	Enemy systematically shelled this locality from 7.30 to NOON with 10.5 m. how. shells in his performance with which – two were accompanied by considerable aerial activity. Only one battery seemed to be employed – not any natural target one time, our road, but 2 guns in a battery 4.00x in front were knocked out.	Rep
		12 M.	Minimal artillery activity on part of enemy nearly 10.5 m. hows on MORCHIES and our transport routes in rally. C.30.b. D.25.a., D.19.c. 4.m.s. (two) fired repeatedly at enemy planes through the day. O.C. reconnoitred intermediate line with D.M.G.D. Sites for additional guns selected – wire to be commenced in implements immediately. Situation quiet all day. 2/LT SADDLETON went on Bgde course.	Rep
"	23/7/17	12 N.	Prepared scheme for staying German post in D.7.c – subject to approval by Bde. and Bgd. in our front line. LT OXLEY-BOYLE went on course. Situation quiet – weather dull and showery – observation from VAUX to enemy line more nightly (from dawn to midnight) to shell our transport routes leading from VAUX to night sub-sector. The Brigade Hun on 22ND INST. on which Day 2/4 D.J.W. REGT. made a relief in daylight over these routes, evidently observed by enemy balloons and O.P's.	Rep
		12 M.		Rep
"	25/7/17	12 N.	Situation quiet. LAGNICOURT shelled intermittently thro' the day with 77 and 105 M. Usual shelling of transport and communications routes after dark. Weather dull.	Rep
"	28/7/17	12 N.	Situation quiet. Our artillery active thro' the morning – no reply so far from Germans.	Rep
"	29/7/17	12 N.	Situation quiet – battery positions in this locality lightly shelled with 10.5 m. about 11 AM. Our transport was shelled last night – no casualties but a mule bolted and has not yet been found.	Rep
"	29/7/17	12 N.	Situation quiet. Orders issued for relief. Missing mule has been found.	Rep
		11 PM	Relieved by 209 M.G. COY. (see APPENDIX IV)	APP 1M.(A) Rep
"	29/7/17	1.25 AM	Relief complete and lay in camp at H.14.a. (57C N.W.)	Rep
		12 N.	On account of rain so rather work could be done – much trouble with us every one attempting to —	Rep

Army Form C. 2118.

213th Machine Gun Coy

WAR DIARY
or
INTELLIGENCE SUMMARY.
(Erase heading not required.)

Place	Date	Hour	Summary of Events and Information	Remarks and references to Appendices
H19a	30/7/17	12 N.	Kit inspection - bath - Pay parade. Weather still unsettled	App 9
—"—	31/7/17	12 N.	Training programme commenced including Range firing but weather too bad for good work	App 9

Rodreque Kruik
H 213 M.G Coy

Copy 2

APP. I
War Diary

213. M.G. Coy.   Order No 1/5
                                    2.7.19
Orders for relief.

Reference map 57.D.N.E.

(1) Relief
(a) The company less No 1 section under 2/Lt. Boyle, will be relieved in the front line by 2 guns of 208 M.G. Coy on the night 4/5 July. Completion of relief to be reported by section officers in person to Coy. H.Q. C.16.b.1.2.
Section on relief will march independently to transport lines BUSSEBOOM H.18.d. where accommodation will be arranged by Lieut. Crosse in the camp vacated by 208 M.G. Coy.
(b) Lieut. Oxley Boyle will remain at C.16.b.1.2. i/c No 1 section with 2 guns in support at C.5.a. & 5 guns in reserve at C.16.b.1.2. When 208 Coy have completed the relief he will report via C.16.b.1.2.

(2) Handing over.
Section officers will hand over tripods, belt, belt boxes S.A.A. grenades, maps, range cards, order boards, defence schemes and all trench stores. Receipts will be obtained for tripods and belt boxes, these will be received over from 208 Coy at transport lines at 11.30 a.m. 5th July.

(3) Guides
Each gun group will detail one guide to meet 208 Coy at road junction C.6.a.u.5. Lieut. Crosse will detail a guide to accompany 208 Coy transport officer to the dump in C.5.c.

(4) Transport
(a) Lieut. Crosse will detail one limber to meet sections at 2.30 a.m. 5th July at rations dump in C.5.c. If relief is delayed and daylight prevents the moving of transport in this locality, then limber will wait at road junction C.16.a.u.5. British front guns and spare parts must be carried. The section in reserve will assist in carrying.
(b) One limber to report to Coy H.Q. C.16.b.1.2, at 11 pm. 4th July to move Coy. H.Q.
(c) Hot tea to be provided Coy on arrival at transport lines.

                                            R.H. Joyce Lieut.
                                            o/c 213 Coy
                                            M.G.C.

                                            Acknowledge

COPY No
1. O/c No 1 Section
2. O/c   " 2
3. O/c   " 3
4. O/c   " 4
5. Lieut Crosse
6. O/c 208 M.G. Coy
7. D.M.G.O.
8. 186 Inf Bde.
9. C.2. M.S.
10. S.C.
11&12. War diary

app II

RELIEF ORDER 213 M.G. Coy No. R.1.

REFERENCE MAPS
57° N.W. & N.E. 1:20000

11 July 1917

Appendix II

1. RELIEF — 213 M.G. Coy will relieve 212 M.G. Coy in the right (LAGNICOURT) section of the line on night of 12/13 July.

2. DETAILS
(a) No 2 Section under Lt. CROSSE will relieve No 2 section of 212 Coy under Lt. COPE in the right sub-section.
(b) Lt. ORLEY-BOYLE & 2/Lt DENT with No 1 Section & 2 guns of No 4 Section will relieve 6 guns of 212 Coy under Lt. SAMPSON in the left sub sector.
(c) Remaining 2 guns of No 4 Section will relieve 2 guns of 212 Coy at C.29.a.1.5 and C.29.d.8.4. These guns to come under supervision of Lt. McFARLANE. relief to be conducted and reported when completed by him.
(d) No 3 Section under Lt. McFARLANE to be in reserve in Coy Hdqrs C.22.d.8.0.
(e) Reliefs to be reported to Coy Hdqrs as soon as completed.

3. TAKING OVER
(a) Coy stores: 213 Coy will take over report and field boxes.
(b) Trench stores: 213 Coy will take over all S.A.A., GRENADES, SIGNALS, TOOLS, MAPS, DEFENCE SCHEMES, ETC. Copy of receipts for (a) & (b) to be handed in to Coy Hdqrs in duplicate by noon 13th July. These to be made up by Section officers from receipts given by N.C.O. i/c each gun team.

4. RATIONS — Rations only (not water) will be taken in by 213 Coy. O.C. M.T. will arrange for teas to be served at 7.30 pm July 12th.

5. COY HDQTS — Section Officers will arrange that at least 2 men in each section know their way to Coy Hdqrs & that all runners in each sec'n know where section Hdqrs are. Coy Hdqrs at C.22.d.8.0. Sunken Road between Copse (Bois-de-VAUX) and LAGNICOURT.

6. GUIDES — 2 guides one for each sub-sector will meet 213 Coy on arrival at C.22.b.6.2. & on arrival at section Hdqrs new guides per gun will be provided.

7. TRANSPORT — Will be under arrangement of 2/Lt CURZON to whom a later order will be issued.

8. ADVANCE PARTY — 2/Lt SADDLETON, A/C.S.M. & 2 signallers will leave for 213 Coy Hdqrs at 5.30 am 12 July.

9. COMPANY PARADE — Coy will parade in fighting order, water bottles full, at 8.30 pm.

10. REPORTS — Casualty reports & intelligence summary to reach Coy Hdqrs by 10 A.M. daily.

COPY Nº
1. O/C Nº 1 Section
2. O/C Nº 2
3. O/C Nº 3
4. O/C Nº 4
5. Lt A.S. GUN SECTION
6. O/C 212 M.G. COY
7. D.M.G.O.
8. 186 INF. BDE
9. O.C. M.G.
10. O. C.S.M.
11. TELE
12. WAR DIARY

O/C 213 Coy
M.G.C.

Secret.   Operation Order   No R.H.3
App III   213 M.G. Coy
War Diary   July 16/917

Reference map. 57-D24. 1:20,000   Appendix III

(1) **Scheme**
185th Infantry Brigade are raiding a german post at about D.13.b.a.3. on the night of the 16/17th. The 213th M.G. Coy on receipt of a code message will bring covering fire to bear on the german line from D.7.d.5.0. to D.13.b.9.0.

(2) **Details**
2 guns of No 3 Section will be under 2/Lt McFarlane for this duty. They will be in position on the ground chosen at about C.18.c.8.4. by 11 p.m. 16th. On receipt of code message fire will be opened at following rate :— 5 belts continuous per gun followed by 3 belts per gun in bursts of 20/50 rounds. At conclusion they will withdraw to Coy Hdqrs.

(3) **Communications**
A wire has been laid from Battn Hdqrs 2/5th D of W to gun position. Lt Crosse will report to O/C 2/5th D of W and hold himself in readiness to give the code word over this wire. O/C 2/5th D of W will give the word to Lt. Crosse when the raiding party is coming in. Code word "KNOCK" — no other message will pass over the wire to the M.G. position.

(4) **Route of retirement**
The raiding party will probably retire to M.L.R. via road and track in C.24.b and therefore will not come directly under the covering fire.

(5) **Carrying party**
A carrying party of 10 men from 186th Bde. T.M.B. will assist 213 M.G Coy in carrying ammunition etc. to positions via DUNELM AVENUE and M.L.R.

(6) **General**
O/C 2/5th and 2/6th D of W have been warned that this firing over their outpost line will take place. Gun team will take shelter in dugout and trench in vicinity of C.m.4.5 before firing and after if necessary.

Copies to.
2/Lt McFarlane
Lt Crosse
186th Inf. Bde.
War Diary (2)
Extra   (2)

R W Joyce Lieut
O/C 213 Coy
M G C

SECRET   RELIEF ORDER 213 M.G. Coy.

Ref. Map 57d NW NE 20,000

Appendix III (a)

(1) 213 M.G. Coy will be relieved the 204 M.G. Coy
Relief   in the right (LACHICOURT) section of the line on the
         night of 28/29 July.

II.   (a) No. 1 Section & 2 guns of No. 2 Section do not at present
Reliefs   in the line. 1 gun will be relieved 1 gun of 204 Coy.
         [illegible further sub-paragraphs]

III.   [illegible — "Standing over"]

IV.   [illegible — "Guides"]

[remainder of page largely illegible]

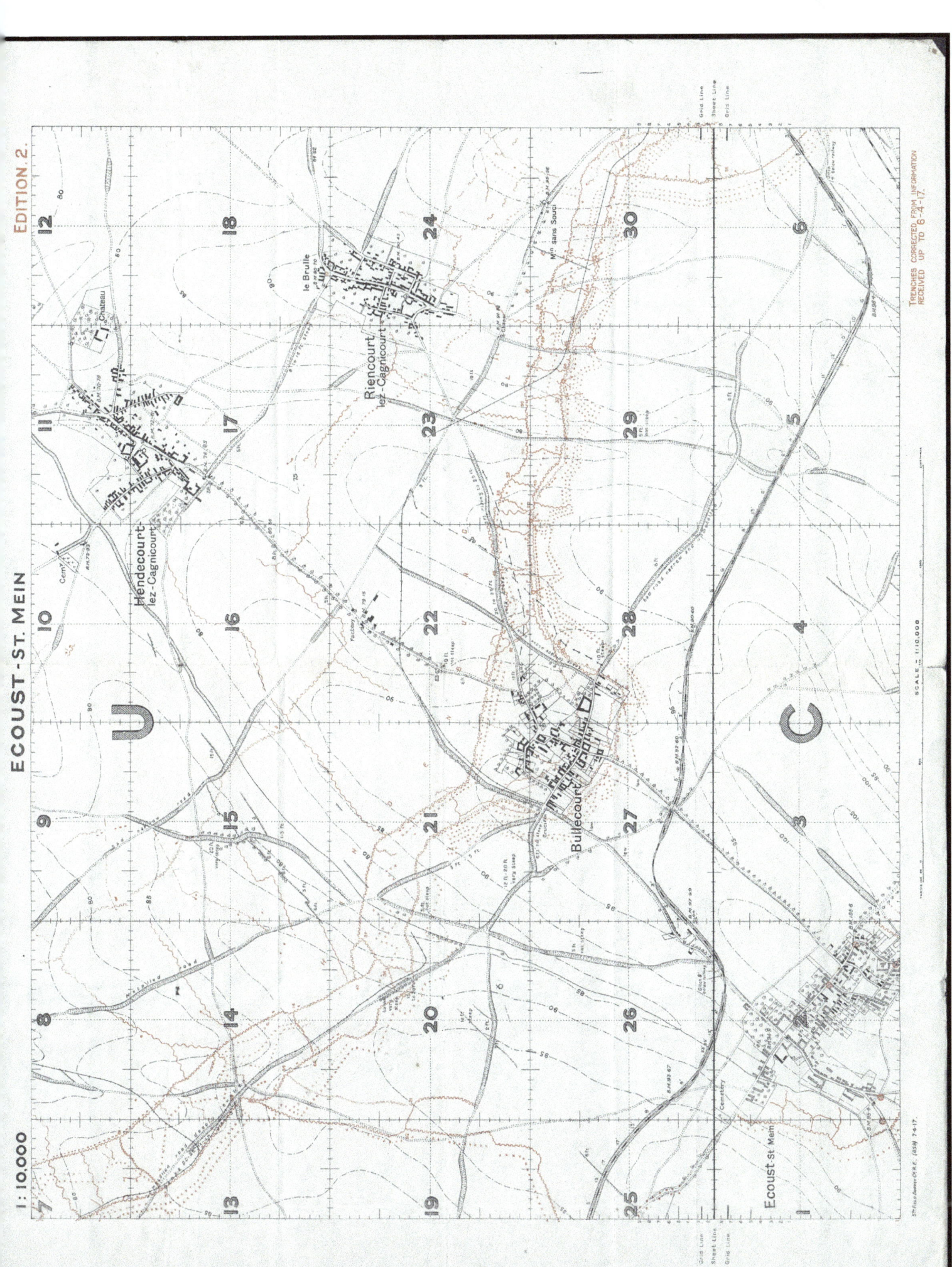

Original

Confidential
Appendix No. 1
War Diary 213 MI Coy
Map ECOUST. ST. MEIN 1/10.000

Original

Secret

W.D. 6

War Diary
of
213th Machine Gun Company

From 1st August 1917 to 31st August 1917

(Volume 6)

Northern Cps.
O/C 213 Coy
M.G.C.

WAR DIARY
or
INTELLIGENCE SUMMARY

Army Form C. 2118.

213 Coy
April-Coy

Place	Date	Hour	Summary of Events and Information	Remarks and references to Appendices
4.18.a. 57c N.W	1/8/17	12.N.	Heavy rain prevented outdoor work. I.A. and Mechanisms done under cover.	R+q
		6.P.M.	Received to relieve 212 Coy in the NOREUIL Sector tomorrow.	
"	2/8/17	12.N.	O.C. and 3 other officers made reconnaissance of front line. Lt. EKINS transferred to 92ND M.G. Coy.	APR. I. R+q
		8.P.M.	Move off to front line (OPER" ORDER R.H.5 APPENDIX I) rain all day	
C.16.c.12 57c N.W	3/8/17	1.25 A.M.	Relief complete but uncomfortable - trenches in bad condition owing to rain.	R+q
		12.N.	Situation quiet	
		8 P.M	2/Lts. GRISDALE and EASTON joined Company from BASE.	
"	4/8/17	12.N.	Situation still quiet.	R+q
		6.P.M	D.M.G.O and O.C. Coy made reconnaissance of new M.G positions as recommended by VI Corps MGO	
"	5/8/17	4 A.M	Reconnaissance resumed - in direction of BULLECOURT.	R+q
		8.P.M	Enemy plane brought down by me of ours - crashed and burnt near RIENCOURT.	
		12.M.	Situation quiet. Weather unsettled.	
"	6/8/17	12.N.	Situation quiet. We are doing a little shooting from box mountings at morning and evening stand to	R+q
"	7/8/17	12.N	Situation very quiet. Suspicious objects reported seen in NOREUIL.	R+q
		10 PM	Enemy put on a 30 minute stage on our left sub sector - minutes and hows. The usual retaliation resulted. Our M.G.s in Coy reserve fired 2000 rounds in wrath in front of QUEANT.	
"	8/8/17	12.N.	Rather more artillery activity than usual.	R+q
		7 P.M	Intense rainfall - trenches and shelters flooded. No 4 section (minimum) retired No 1 m. 11.29.f.	
"	9/8/17	12.N.	Some artillery activity. This is more general, the Boche appears to have at most 3 batteries which he can switch about. His shooting however intense, is invariably on a small area. Two M.G.s	R+q
			and snipers are always firing about thro' the hours of stand to. Weather wet and cool.	
		9.P.M	A heavy bombardment broke out on our left which lasted one hour - at this time 12 of our	
			planes were seen moving towards that direction.	
"	10/8/17	12.N	Situation quiet	R+q
"	11/8/17	12.N.	Relieved by 208 Coy. Relief complete at 3.30 a.m. See September II	R+q APR.II.

Army Form C. 2118.

WAR DIARY
or
INTELLIGENCE SUMMARY.
(Erase heading not required.)

2/3 Coy
An G.C.

Instructions regarding War Diaries and Intelligence Summaries are contained in F.S. Regs., Part II. and the Staff Manual respectively. Title pages will be prepared in manuscript.

Place	Date	Hour	Summary of Events and Information	Remarks and references to Appendices
B.18.b S.7C.N.W	12/8/17	12 N	Day given up to cleaning and inspection	Ref
"	13/9/17	12 N	Machine gun training commences	Ref
"	14/6/17	12 N	Daily training continues Bath parade	Ref
"	15/8/17	12 N	" " Inoculation 50% on men. Bomb a BAPAUME	Ref
"	16/8/17	12 N	" 2nd Lt ___ proceeded to 173 Coy M.G.C.	Ref
"	17/8/17	12 N	" 2nd Lt MULLIGAN with 4 O.R.'s made reconnaissance and struck off Coy	Ref
"	18/8/17	12 N	O.C. and 2 other officers made reconnaissance of BULLECOURT	Ref
"	19/8/17	12 N	O.M and 2 others at " & B/Lt in BULLECOURT sect today	Ref APRIL
B.17.b S.7C.N.W	20/9/17	1.30 AM	See Reports III Relief complete	Ref
"	"	12 N	Situation quiet	Ref
"	21/9/17	12 N	Situation quiet. Owing to the changing of guns (in accordance with Corps M.G. Officer's scheme) there was so little machine gun activity as to positions + S.O.S. lines that no new firing returns today.	Ref
"	22/8/17	12 N	Situation abnormally quiet from a machine gun stand point - arrangements for manning guns etc as per M5	Ref
"	23/9/17	12 N	Lt. O'L EY BOYLE reported back from course. Situation quiet	Ref
"	24/9/17	12 N	Situation quiet - weather conditions. Some rifle firing too.	Ref
"	25/8/17	12 N	Situation quiet to enemy artillery and trench mortar increasing slightly daily.	Ref

LT. R.A.T. MILLER firing company OC Mg

Army Form C. 2118.

WAR DIARY
or
INTELLIGENCE SUMMARY

213 Coy
M.G.C.

(Erase heading not required.)

Place	Date	Hour	Summary of Events and Information	Remarks and references to Appendices
B17 6 & S7C N.W	26/8/17	12N	Situation quiet	
"	27/8/17	12N	Situation quiet. 1 casualty and one gun slightly damaged	
"	28/8/17	12N	Situation quiet. Our night firing draws more retaliation than formerly and enemy trench mortars are very active and accurate on front line near BULLECOURT Rly J	
"	29/8/17	12N		
"	30/8/17	12N	Situation quiet. The unsettled weather of the past week has prevented any Artillery activity.	
"	31/8/17	12N		

R.A. Annie Capt
OC 213 MG Coy.

1/9/17

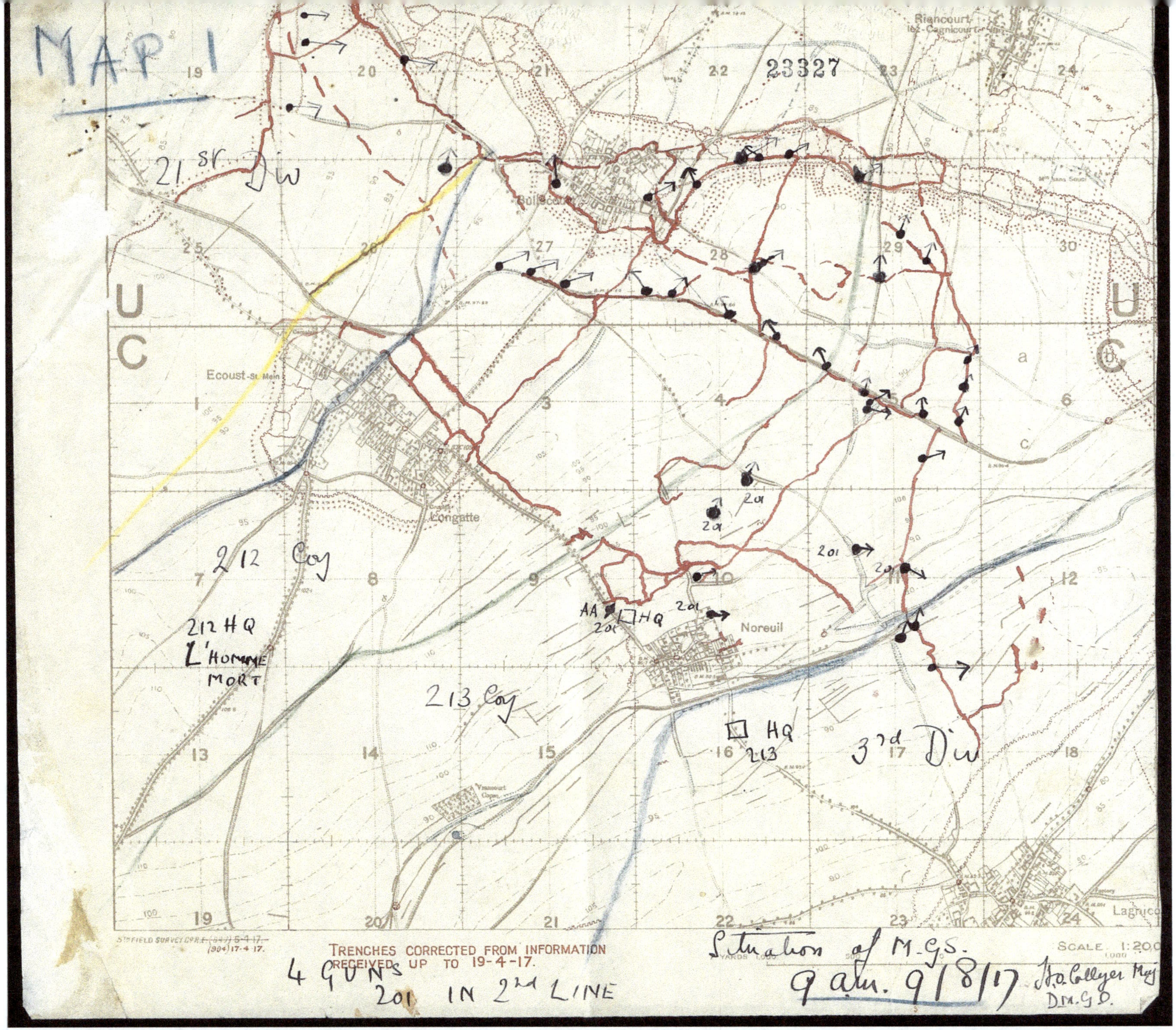
MAP I
23327
Riencourt-lez-Cagnicourt
Bullecourt
Ecoust-St Mein
Longatte
Noreuil
Lagnicourt
21st Div
212 Coy
212 HQ
L'HOMME MORT
213 Coy
HQ
213
3rd Div
AA
201
TRENCHES CORRECTED FROM INFORMATION RECEIVED UP TO 19-4-17.
SCALE 1:20,000
YARDS 1,000 500 0 1,000
4 GUNS 201 IN 2nd LINE
Situation of M-GS.
9 am. 9/8/17
H.O. Collyer Maj
DMGO.

SECRET. Operation Order   R.H.5
        213 M.G. Coy.
                                                    Aug 2/1917
Reference Maps 57° N.W. 1:20,000
                Special Sheet 1:10,000 (57° S.W. S.E. & 57° N.W. N.E.)

Relief   213 M.G. Coy will relieve 212 M.G. Coy in
        the Left (NOREUIL) Sector of the front line on night of
II   2/3 August
        (a) No.1 Section less 1 gun under Lieut Saddleton
            will relieve Lt. Cope (Positions A1, A2, A3)
        (b) No.2 Section less 1 gun under Lt Cross will
            relieve Lt. Sampson (Positions D1, D2, D3)
        (c) No.3 Section & 1 gun of No.2 Section under 2/Lt.
            Fortune will relieve Lt Williams (
             , D1, D2, D3.)
        (d) No.4 Section & 1 gun of No.1 Section under 2/Lt.
            Wilkinson will be in reserve at Coy Hdqrs
        (e) Completion of relief will be reported to Coy Hdqrs

III   213 Coy will take over bipods, belts, S.A.A.
Taking over Grenades & all trench stores including Maps & defence
        schemes. Each Section Officer will send in to Coy
        Hdqrs a list of what has been taken over by 12 noon Aug 3

IV   212 Coy will provide guides to meet 213 Coy at C.16.a.4.5.
Guides at 10.30 pm.

V   All reports to reach Coy Hdqrs by 9 A.M. daily.
Reports Section Hdqrs at C.6.a (Lt. Cross) will be a relay
        station where all messages to and from the advanced
        sections will be relayed

VI   In sunken road C.16.b.1.2
Coy Hqrs

VII   Operation orders will be given to T.O.s
Transport

VIII   (a) Coy will parade at 8.00 p.m. Dress fighting
General   order. Rain coats will be worn, shovel, equipment,
            water bottle filled.
        (b) Q.M.S. will have hot tea served at 7.15 pm.

Copy No.
No.1 O/C No.1 Section
  2   O/C No.2   "
  3   O/C No.3   "
  4   O/C No.4   "
  5   2/C / Aslt Militon   R.W.Tryon Lieut
  6   O/C 212 Coy   O/C 213 Coy
  7   186th Inf Bde
  8   D.M.G.O.
  9   File
10&11 War Diary

213 M.G. Coy
WAR DIARY
Aug 1-31, 1917

Appendix I

SECRET

OPERATION ORDER No. R.H6

213 Machine Gun Coy.

REFERENCE MAP 57C NW 1:20000

1. RELIEF — The Coy will be relieved in the NOREUIL sector on the night of the 11/12 August by 208 M.G. Coy.

2. HEADQTRS — Coy Hdqts will close at present location C.16.b.2.4. at 10.30 p.m. 11 inst. and open at new Coy Hdqts of 201 M.G. Coy, ie. present Coy Hdqts Coy Hdqts on NOREUIL-LONGATTE road 57C NW at same time. This location can be reached by continuing on SYDNEY AVENUE instead of coming out of LOUVRE CORNER.

3. GUIDES — One guide per gun team will meet 208 Coy at relay cnr (No 4 Section Hdqts) at 9.30 pm.

4. TRANSPORT — Transport Officer will send 2 limbers to C.16.b.2.4. to move Coy Hdqts and section in reserve there. 2 limbers of 208 Coy will arrive and be sent to Coy. H.C. corner and draw-ing station to bring out guns of Nos 2, 3 and 4 sections.

5. HANDING OVER — 213 Coy will hand over all belt boxes, hypos, Stens, grenades, picks, shovels, petrol tins, all R.E. material and ammunition. Also all maps and code sheets. Receipts to be handed in to Coy Hdqts by incoming O.C.

6. GENERAL — Nos 4, 5 & 6 sections will take to trenches where possible.

Sections on relief will march independently to point of W.p.a.

C.Q.M.S. will arrange hot tea for Coy on arrival. "RELIEF COMPLETE" to be reported by section officers in person at Coy. Hdqts.

7. ACKNOWLEDGE.

COPIES TO
1. O.C. No 1 Section
2. O.C. No 2 "
3. O.C. No 3 "
4. O.C. No 4 "
5. 2/i.c. & Q.S. Coy
6. O.C. 208 M.G. Coy
7. 156th INF. BDE
8. D.H.Q.
9. FILE
10. ✓ WAR DIARY
11./12. SPARE

R.H. Boyce Lieut
O.C.
M.G.C.

213 M.G. Coy
WAR DIARY
Aug 1 - 31. 1917
Appendix II

213 M.C.Coy
OPERATION ORDER.
COPY Nº 10

213 M.G. Coy.
WAR. DIARY.
Aug 1ˢᵗ – 31ˢᵗ 1917.
APPENDIX III

Vol 7

Secret.
War Diary
of
213th M.G. Coy

Volume 7

From 1st Sept 1917   to Sept 1917

R. Mark Capt
Cmdg 213 M.G. Coy

Army Form C. 2118.

WAR DIARY
or
INTELLIGENCE SUMMARY.
(Erase heading not required.)

213 M.G. Coy

Place	Date	Hour	Summary of Events and Information	Remarks and references to Appendices
B.9 & Onward	1/9/17	12 noon	Situation quiet. Enemy T.M's active. Very little enemy artillery. Six M.G. swept back at M.O.R.D.E.N.T.R. (U/7C.) throughout the night.	OTTLE
"	2/9/17	"	Situation normal. M.G. fire (U.6.C.7.2.– U.12.B.50.– U.12.B.45.–O.) were kept under our M.G. fire throughout the night. Relieved by Lt. S.O. Co. going by from M.G. Base Depot.	OTTLE
"	3/9/17	"	Situation quiet. A heavy barrage was put down by our artillery in the direction of Fontaine 2–130–Croisielles at from 7–8 P.M.	OTTLE
"	4/9/17	"	Situation very quiet. 213 M.G. Coy. were relieved in the night of 4.5.5 by the 102nd M.G. Coy.	APPÉ 49'A L OTTLE
H.182 Cent.	5/9/17	"	Coy in rest. Morning devoted to cleaning up of men & equipment, and in the afternoon inspection of GAS helmets.	OTTLE
"	6/9/17	9—10 A.M. 2—4:30 P.M.	Inf. Drill, Musketry & fire control Immediate action. T.O.E.T., Combined Drill.	OTTLE
"	7/9/17	9—12:30 P.M. 2:30—4:30 P.M.	Infantry Drill, Immediate action. Practised fire Direction. Continuation of same.	OTTLE
"	8/9/17	9—12:30 P.M. 2—	Tactical Exercise, T.O.E.T. Baths.	OTTLE
"	9/9/17		Capt R.H. Brice Transferred to 201 M.G. Coy. as additional Capt – Capt L.A. ROMAN transferred from 201 M.G. Coy. to 213 M.G. Coy. to this Company. Authority A.G. No. A/13553/16 of 5-9-17. Coy inspected by Capt L.A ROMAN.	OTTLE

Army Form C. 2118.

WAR DIARY
or
INTELLIGENCE SUMMARY.
(Erase heading not required.)

213 M.G. Coy

Place	Date	Hour	Summary of Events and Information	Remarks and references to Appendices
H.B.Q. Cotur	10/9/17	9–12:30 2–4:30	Range Practice. Lt Gilbert of Div Gas Officer at Div Gas School.	O.H.W.
"	11/9/17	5–2:30	Brigade Route march. The Brigade was inspected on the march by the Divisional & Brigade Commanders.	O.H.W.
"	12/9/17	9:030	Infield & Bayonet fighting and Gas. This afternoon 4 sub Coy went to Batn. Billets night of Dec 12/13. 213 M.G. Coy relieved 212 M.G. Coy in the R. Section.	APPENDIX O.H.W.
	13/9/17	4.A.M.	At 4 A.M. enemy put down a heavy barrage of shells & Trench mortars immediately after APEX. Guns of this unit responded immediately. S.O.S. signal which was reported to have gone up & continued firing until artillery pushed heavy. It appears that the enemy attempted a raid with a party of about 30 by entering the trench between two of the posts which held out throughout the whole engagement & were never reached. Enemy raids a number of them. The remainder of the day was very quiet.	O.H.W.
	14/9/17	12 noon	Situation quiet. Intermittent shelling by Enemy throughout day & night. WW2 carried out re hostile Barrage Sets at night. 2nd Lt GRESPIGE wounded in the leg whilst visiting one of the nests. 1 our sent down the line to Base.	O.H.W.
	15/9/17	12 noon	Situation quiet. Intermittent shelling of YPRES CORNER throughout the night by air craft very active watching enemy lines. 2nd Lt A.K. STIRLING reported from M.G. Base D.pot to duty. 2nd Lt D. MILLIKIN reported Coy from HOSPITAL. A/M.W.H. SADLER struck off strength. To Base hospital.	O.H.W.

16/9/17

Army Form C. 2118.

WAR DIARY
or
INTELLIGENCE SUMMARY.
(Erase heading not required.)

213 K. M.G. Coy

Instructions regarding War Diaries and Intelligence Summaries are contained in F. S. Regs., Part II. and the Staff Manual respectively. Title pages will be prepared in manuscript.

Place	Date	Hour	Summary of Events and Information	Remarks and references to Appendices
NOREUIL	16/9/17	12 noon	Heavy barrage opened & be put down by us in the direction of FONTAINE-LES-CROISELLES at 9.30pm. Heavy machine gun fire could also be distinguished on our front situation any quiet. Weather continued on not & Barrage site situation normal. Intermittent shelling by our artillery throughout day & night.	OH4u
NOREUIL	17.9.17	12 noon	Enemy shelled IGAREE CORNER & NOREUIL valley during the night with 10.5 & 15 c.m shells. One enemy plane crossed our lines & was driven off with A.A. fire.	OH4u
NOREUIL	18/9/17	12 noon	Our artillery fires crashes throughout the night. 7 M.G. fired 20 belts into Companies with artillery crashes. Observer situation quiet.	OH4u
NOREUIL	19/9/17	12 noon	Situation normal a good deal of aerial activity on both sides. No report the day enemy machines engaged by M.G. fire.	OH4u
NOREUIL	20/9/17	12 noon	Enemy attempted raid at 4.15 A.M. but was dispersed by Artillery & M.G. fire in open ground. 2/Lt. Spencer reports decrease in strength.	N/I
NOREUIL	21.9.17		Artillery previous shelled through truck minor action in the neighbourhood of the APEX and in the vicinity of nº 18 gun. Emplacement shaken but no damage done. Test carried out by our M.G. fire on their S.O.S. lines. Results satisfactory though no observation was obtained.	EJ
NOREUIL	22.9.17		Situation normal Enemy aircraft more active. Four Hunnel and engaged by our M.G. LA fam. Further hots of 200 holes carried out. Stable noº 19 turn gun from S.I.R. by who took over 702 76A on 21.9.17	N/I

N Bryan Capt.
Comdg 213 m.g.g

WAR DIARY or INTELLIGENCE SUMMARY

Army Form C. 2118.

213th M.G. Coy

Place	Date	Hour	Summary of Events and Information	Remarks and references to Appendices
NOREUIL	23/9/17		Bombardment of APEX by heavy T.M's from 9.0 - 9.30pm Activity by E.A's above normal. General situation unchanged. Punishing A.St 9's etc. lines carried out.	A.P.
NOREUIL	24/9/17		Situation generally normal. Punishing shoots carried out throughout day by our artillery and T.M's. Own m/gs fired approx. 10,000 rounds in conjunction with our artillery. 5500 rounds fired by m/gs who were overhead near BERTINCOURT. M/gs were to be dropping bombs.	A.P.
NOREUIL	25/9/17		Weather fine. Situation quiet with the exception of a certain amount of hostile T.M activity in the neighbourhood of R.APEX Own m/gs fired 2500 rounds on back areas - conjunction with own artillery at night. Aerial activity normal.	A.P.
NOREUIL	26/9/17		Combined action between our artillery, m/gs + T.M's arranged to simulate an attack and carried out between 5.30 and 6 hr. Enemy retaliated by shelling + trench mortaring the APEX. Own m/gs fired 5000 rounds. Remainder of day quiet. Weather fine.	A.P.

A. Green Capt.
Comdg 213 M.G. Coy

Army Form C. 2118.

WAR DIARY
or
INTELLIGENCE SUMMARY.
(Erase heading not required.)

213th M.G. Coy

Place	Date	Hour	Summary of Events and Information	Remarks and references to Appendices
NOREUIL	27.9.17		Weather fine. General situation quieter than normal. T.M. activity on both sides near the APEX. Arrange about relief of 208 Bry. up to App no 3 by O.O. no 10 issued	App no 3
NOREUIL	28.9.17		Weather fine. Situation unchanged. Relief by C.O. & Coy. Complete by 12 midnight. Training programme drawn up	App no 4
NOREUIL	29.9.17		Day spent in cleaning up equipment gun material also checking same	
NOREUIL	30.9.17		Sunday. Kit inspection. Pack ordnance issue App no 5.	App no 5

[Signature] Capt.
Comdg 213 M.G. Coy.

2/3rd M. G. Coy

APPENDIX

Nº 1

September 1917

Operation Order by Capt R.S. Joyce
Commanding 2/3rd M.G. Coy   No R.N

Reference Maps. 57C NW 1:20,000
Special Tracing

(1) RELIEF The Company will be relieved in the BULLECOURT sector of the front line, by 208th M.G. Coy on the night of the 4th/5th.

(2) DETAILS
(a) Each Section on relief will, on completion of same, by runner direct to Coy. H.Q. & will then march independently to camp at H.18.a.
(b) No. 1 Section at the Abbey MORY on relief will report completion of same by runner to Coy H.Q. & march direct to Camp without further orders.
(c) "A" Group (5 guns) & "B" Group (2 guns) will be relieved by 7 guns 208 Coy, these to be embussed at end of TANK AVE C.w.d. The limber carrying these guns will drop the 2 guns which relieve "D" Group at the camouflage on the road at O.y.c.central, & on return will pick up the 2 guns of 2/3 Coy at same place.
(d) "E" Group (2 guns) & "C" Group (3 guns) will be relieved by 5 guns of 208 Coy, to be embussed at O.o.c. road in M.3.c. by railway embankment. This limber will bring out 2/3 Coy (5 guns).

(3) GUIDES Mounted guides will go with 208 Coy to embussing points, where one guide per gun will be provided.

(4) HANDING OVER 2/3 Coy will hand over all hostile stores including tripods, belts, & S.A.A., also all maps, barrage tables & defence schemes. Receipts for these to be handed in to Coy H.Q. by noon 5th inst.
PETROL TINS — A full tin will be left on each gun position for use in lieu of water. All other tins will be brought out.

(5) TRANSPORT Transport Officer 2/3 Coy will have limbers at Coy H.Q. at 9.00 p.m. & a mess cart for use of H.Q. staff.

(6) GENERAL On going from the overland route, avoid tracks where possible. O.C. Coys will meet Company at camp.

(7) ACKNOWLEDGE by each officer at head of list by the word "CORRECT".

R.S. Joyce Capt
O.C. 2/3 Coy

Copies:
1. O.C. No 1 Section   (8) 1st INF. BDE
2. " No 2 "   (8) D.M.G.O
3. " No 3 "
4. " No 4 "   " WAR DIARY
5. " A.S.C Section
6. O.C. 208 M.G. Coy.   " SPARE

213 K McEvoy
APPENDIX
No 2

September 1917

SECRET   213th Machine Gun Company   Copy No 3

Operation Order No 9

Reference Map 51^B SW 4 1/10,000   H.G.F.
            57^C NW 2 1/10,000

1. On the night of the 12th/13th inst 213th M.G. Coy will relieve 212th M.G. Coy in the right section

2. The disposition and designation of the guns to be relieved are as follows:—

    M 1   C 11 b 1.1 ⎫
    M 2   C 11 b 2.9 ⎬ Right Group
    M 3   C 5 d 3.4 ⎭

    M 4   C 5 d 8.7 ⎫
    M 5   C 5 d 2.9 ⎬ Centre Group
    M 6   C 5 a 3.3 ⎭
    A 1   U 29 b 4.0

    I 1   C 10 c 9.6 ⎫
    I 2   C 10 a 80.05 ⎬ Intermediate
    I 3   C 10 a 80.05 ⎬ line
    I 4   C 10 a 9.5 ⎭
    D 1   C 9 b 50.45 N^r Coy HQ

1 A.A. Gun at Coy HQ C 11 d 7.7

3 Guns in Brigade Reserve near Bde H.Q. C 26 c 80.75

3. The groups will be relieved as follows:—

Right Group (Commander 2nd Lt. J.H. GRISDALE) No 1 Section (less 1 gun)

Centre Group ("   Lt. R.F. OXLEY-BOYLE) No 4 Section

Intermediate ("   2nd Lt J McFARLANE) (No 3 Section and 1 gun of No 1 Section)

    AA Gun Coy HQ   1 Gun of No 2 Section

Brigade Reserve (Commander 2nd Lt. E.W. DENT) No 2 Section less 1 gun

4. The following material ONLY will be taken over

    Trench Stores
    Tripods

over

cont:

        10 belt boxes per position
        2 petrol cans per position

Lists of material taken over will be forwarded by Group Commanders to Coy H.Q. by 12 noon on 13/5/17. No material of any description will be taken over by the Section in reserve

<u>5</u> 1 Guide from centre and 3 Guides from intermediate Groups will be at IGAREE CORNER at 9.15 pm
  1 Guide from right Group will be at the Crater C 10 c. 9. 5. 10 at 9.15 pm
  1 Guide from D 1 gun will be at Coy H.Q at 9 pm
  1   " " Reserve Section will be at T. 1. b. u.u. at 6 pm

<u>6</u>(a) 1 limber, containing the Centre Group gun material in fore portion and intermediate Group gun material less D 1 gun in rear portion, will proceed to IGAREE CORNER where the rear portion will be unhooked

The fore portion will then move with the Guide of the Centre Group to M 5 position where it will be unloaded. It will then return to IGAREE CORNER pick up its rear portion and wait for the gun material of Nos 1 & 2 Sections of 212 Coy which it will bring back to camp

(b) 1 half limber will have the gun material of the Right Group and after picking up the Guide proceed to HOBART CROSS C 4 c. 7. 7. where it will unload and wait for the gun material of 212 M. G. Coy which it will bring back to camp

(c) 2 limbers will be required for H.Q and D 1 and the A.A. guns. These limbers will proceed direct to Coy. H.Q.

(d) The full transport of the section in reserve will proceed to VAULX where it will remain during

<u>over</u>

Cont.

...... of the Company on the line

7. The greatest care will be exercised by Group Commanders in taking over positions, full information being obtained regarding

    Tactical positions of guns
    Barrage and battle lines
    Range Cards
    Work in hand and proposed

8. Completion of all reliefs will be reported to Coy. H.Q. by code word "AGAIN ..... P.M / A.M"

9. ACKNOWLEDGE

Issued by hand at 9 A.M. 12/9/17

                    O.K.Miller.
                    Lt and Adjt.
                    213th M.G. Company

1. File
2/3 War Diary
4 - No 1 Section
5 " 2 "
6 " 3 "
7 " 4 "
8 Transport "
9 C.d.s.
10 62 M.S.
11 212 M.G.Coy
12 186th Inf Bde

213th M.G. Coy

APPENDIX

No 3

September 1917

SECRET   213ᵗʰ Machine Gun Company   COPY NO. 3
                         Operation Order No. 10

Reference Map 51ᴮ S.W. 1/10.000   27.9.17
               57ᶜ N.W. 1/10.000

1   The 213ᵗʰ M.G. Coy will be relieved by the
208ᵗʰ M.G. Coy on the night of the 28ᵗʰ/29ᵗʰ inst.

2   The designation, location and administrative
grouping of the guns is as follows:—
        18   U 29 b 4.0 ⎫ APEX
        19   U 29 a 05.95 ⎭ GROUP

        22(1) C 5 d 6.7   ⎫
        22(2) C 5 d 2.9   ⎬ CENTRE GROUP
        24   C 5 a 3.3   ⎭

        20   C 11 b 1.1 ⎫
        21(1) C 11 b 2.9 ⎬ RIGHT GROUP
        21(2) C 5 d 3.4   ⎭

        20A   C 10 c 9.6 ⎫
        16   C 10 a 8.0 ⎬ INTERMEDIATE
        23A   C 10 a 7.1 ⎬ GROUP
        25A   C 10 a 5.6 ⎭

    1 A.A. Gun at Coy H.Q., C 9 d 7.7.
    1 Section less 1 Gun in Bde Reserve near
    Bde H.Q. C 26 c 80.75.

3   At each gun position in the above groups
              French Stove
              Tripods
              Belt boxes
will be handed over. This includes the tactical &
standing orders & boards.
    At all gun positions the inventory boards will
                                                (over)

(2)

be completed & signed & in addition a list of material handed over will be drawn up & receipted. This list will be forwarded to Coy H.Q. by 12 noon on 29.9.17.

  At Coy H.Q. & at VAULX no gun material will be handed over.

4 (a) One guide from each of the following positions will be at the railway cutting C.5.d.2.9. at 8.15 p.m.
   18, 19, 22(1), 22(2) & 24.

(b) One guide from each of the following positions will be at HOBART CROSS at 8.15 p.m.
   20, 21(1), & 21(2)

(c) One guide from each of the following positions will be at IGAREE CORNER at 8 p.m.
   20A, 16, 23A, 25A.

  Each guide will be in possession of a slip of paper stating from which position he comes.

5 The relief of the Section in VAULX will be arranged direct between O/C 208 M.G. Coy & the Section Commander. In the event of O/C 208 Coy deciding not to relieve this section, it will be withdrawn at 7 p.m. return to camp.

6 (a) The limber of 208 Coy bringing up the guns for the RIGHT GROUP will wait at HOBART CROSS & bring out the gun material of 213 Coy.

(b) The limber of 208 Coy bringing up the guns for the APEX, CENTRE, & INTERMEDIATE GROUPS will unhook their rear portion, packed with the INTERMEDIATE GROUP guns, at IGAREE CORNER, the fore portion packed with the APEX & CENTRE GROUPS guns moving on to the railway cutting. This limber will wait & bring out the gun material of 213 Coy picking up its rear portion on its way out.

(c) Each Group Commander will detail 1 man to come out with the limbers on which their material is packed.

(d) 2 limbers will be detailed by Transport Officer 213 Coy to bring out H.Q. material. These limbers will report to Coy H.Q. at 8.30 p.m.

          (up)

(3)

7. The greatest care must be exercised in order to ensure that at each position all information regarding tactical position of gun, the S.O.S and battle line, orders for firing is properly handed over. This applies not only to gun commanders but also to Group Commanders.

Information regarding work in hand must also be explained.

8. On relief teams will move back to camp independently after reporting to their Group commanders, & again reporting their arrival in camp to 2/LT EASTON.

9. Relief will reported to Coy H.Q. by the word "FELIX" the message being sent in the Group Commanders name.

10. ACKNOWLEDGE.

Issued by hand at 8.55pm

L. Shaw Capt.
Comdg 213rd M.G. Coy.

1 File
2/3 War Diary
4 2/Lt McFARLANE
5 " MILLIKIN
6 " STIRLING
7 " SPENCER
8 " EASTON
9 " GULSTON
10 C.S.M.
11 C.Q.M.S.
12 208 M.G.COY.
13 186TH INF. BDE.

2/3th M.G. Coy
APPENDIX
No 4

September 1917

Training Programme 213th M.G. Coy

Date	morning				afternoon	
	8.30 to 9.30	9.30 to 10.30	10.30 to 11.30	11.30 to 12.30	2 to 3	3 to 4	4 to 5
29:9:17	Cleaning up - Clothing inspection & exchange Checking Gun equipment Rostho Pay					
30:9:17	Kit & Bivouac Inspection					
1:10:17	Rifle exercises Squad drill	Gun drill	J.A.	"Lecture" Reception French Prisoners	Gas drill	Recreational training
2:10:17	Company drill	Mechanism training	Visual training	Lecture on S.O.S & fixed fire lines	Gun drill	Recreational training
3:10:17	Squad drill including Guard mounting	Elementary map reading	Practical Demonstration of laying guns on indicators, the, company gun's test & clinometer methods		J.A.	Packing & washing limbers
4:10:17	ROUTE MARCH					
5:10:17	Company drill	2 Sections Range "C"	Gun drill Gas drill	J.A.	Gun drill	Gas drill
6:10:17	Rifle exercises squad drill				2 Sections Range "C"	

213th M.G. Coy.
APPENDIX
No 5

September 1917

Company Routine Orders   Copy No 3
by Capt. C. Pollak
Commanding 215th M.G. Company

14th September 1917

No 1. Company Routine Orders.
  C.R.Os are being instituted in order
to facilitate the transmission of instructions to
those concerned. All recipients of these orders
will carefully file their copies for reference,
as from time to time it may be necessary
to refer to an order already issued, when the
number of the order & the date of its publication
only will be quoted.

No 2. Anti Gas Equipment.
  All ranks are reminded that when East
of a line through C.27.c.00, CRUCIFIX - Cross road
C.26.c.8.5 SUGAR FACTORY — B.17.b.2.1.- L'HOMME MORT
both the P.H. & small box respirator must
be carried, the latter in the alert position. Under
no circumstances whatsoever will the P.H. helmet
be removed, but when engaged on working parties,
Officers may at their discretion allow the box
respirator to be removed & placed quite close
to the spot at which the man is working. This
permission however, should be given sparingly
owing to the great danger which is every day
increasing through the use of gas shells by
the enemy. The practice of removing the anti-
gas equipment when going to the latrines must
cease. These instructions apply equally to
those troops employed at Coy & Section H.Q.
amongst whom considerable slackness at present
exists.

No 3. Steel Helmets

All Officers & other ranks whether on duty or off duty are to wear steel helmets north and east of a line drawn through C.27.C.0.0., C.26 central, C.19. central, B.18. central, to B.11 central.

No 4 Messages & Reports

All messages & reports will be sent on the A.F.C 2121, pads of which may be had on application to Coy H Q. Messages will be written in accordance with the instructions laid down in Field Service Regulations, care must be taken that all messages are numbered dated, & timed, the number of the message will consist of the senders initials, followed by the numbers of the message which must run consecutively. Messages will be inclosed in a service envelope A.F.C.398, the spaces outside of which must be properly completed.

The above applies to all the usual correspondence such as situation reports, work reports, casualty reports, & messages. Reports of particular cases may be forwarded on the A.B. 153 in which case all the regulations dealing with official correspondence must be observed.

No 5 Secret messages

Messages marked secret will invariably be acknowledged, the signing of the envelope does not constitute an acknowledgement which will be forwarded in the form of a message on an A.F.C 2121.

J W Garland
2nd Lieut & Adjt
213th M.G. Coy.

Company Routine Orders   Copy No. 3
    by Capt. L. A. Pollak.
Cmdg 213th M. G. Coy.

                          22 Sept 1917

No 6. <u>Cutting of wood.</u>

     Damage has been caused to Woods & Forests in the Third Army Area by the indiscriminate cutting of wood by Units and individuals without reference either to the owners or to higher authority.

     Wood can only be cut after the necessary arrangements have been made with the owners by the Forest Control Officer, Third Army.

     All applications to cut wood for fuel will be referred through Corps and Divisional Hdqrs for Corps and Divisional Troops. Applications to cut wood for Engineer purposes will be referred through C. R. E's and C. E's to the Forest Control Officer Third Army.

     It is forbidden to cut wood in the Third Army Area until application has been made, and sanction received, as above.

No 7 <u>Guns Vickers 303"– Boxes, tin, Luminous Sights.</u>

     The above have been introduced for use with the Luminous Sights for Vickers Guns, and will be issued on a scale of one per set of Luminous Sights.

     The box, which is made of tin plate, is described in para 18581 List of Changes, dated June, 1917. It will be carried in the case spare parts box.

     Indents should be submitted to O.Os concerned, & issue will be made as supplies become available.

No 8. Return of French Inhabitants.

As French Inhabitants are now returning to the Villages West of the ARRAS — ACHIET-LE-GRAND RAILWAY, and they are bringing cattle with them, it is forbidden to cut, or graze horses on, any of the patches of lucerne or clover lying West of the above-mentioned Railway, as all the available lucerne and clover is required for the cattle.

Divisions and independent Units are responsible for seeing that the above order is carried out, by wiring in the lucerne and clover patches if necessary.

No 9. Clinometers - Issue of to M.G. Coys and M.G. Squadrons.

Approval is given for the scale of issue of Clinometers for M.G. Coys and M.G. Squadrons to be increased to one per two guns.

Indents should be submitted through the usual channels, and issue will be made as supplies become available.

Authority.— Q.M.G. 17 (2A3), dated 13/9/17-0/30/36

C.W.T. Miller. Lieut & Adjt.
213th An.G. Coy

Secret

War Diary
of
213th Machine Gun Coy

Vol 8

From 1st October 1917 to 31st October 1917

(Volume 8)

[signature]
Cmdg 213 M Gun Coy.

Army Form C. 2118.

WAR DIARY
or
INTELLIGENCE SUMMARY.

213th Machine Gun Company

(Erase heading not required.)

Instructions regarding War Diaries and Intelligence Summaries are contained in F. S. Regs., Part II and the Staff Manual respectively. Title pages will be prepared in manuscript.

Place	Date	Hour	Summary of Events and Information	Remarks and references to Appendices
BEUGNATRE	1.10.17		Company in Divisional Reserve. Training Carried out according to Programme. GSO1 visited Camp and watched Company at Training. Weather fine	G.P.
BEUGNATRE	2.10.17		Training Carried out according to programme. Officers and NCO's saw aeroplane photos and panorama. Weather fine. DMGO visited.	G.P.
BEUGNATRE	3.10.17		Training carried out according to Programme. Weather fine.	G.P.
BEUGNATRE	4.10.17		Training Carried out according to programme. Information received that Harassing fire (two artillery) would be delivered by 3rd Division (Divl artillery) 9 to 10 pm, 12.10.17 & 6.15 to 7 am 5.10.17. Weather cold and windy. Vickers S.A.A. with reference to relief guns 213.MGCoy	G.P.
BEUGNATRE	5.10.17		Training Carried out according to Programme. Vickers 208 M.G.Coy with reference to relief on 6/7/5 inst. Weather cold and windy. Operation Order No 11 issued.	G.P. Appx I
BEUGNATRE	6.10.17		Morning spent in preparing for going into the line. Relief of 1st Sqno of 20 M.G.Coy by 4 guns of 5/2 M.E.Coy carried out satisfactorily. Weather wet until 5 pm then cleared up.	G.P.
MOREUIL	7.10.17		General situation quiet. Harassing fire carried out by our guns during the night. One Vickers during the morning, heavy rain in afternoon & evening	G.P.

Major
Comdg 213 M.G.Coy

Army Form C. 2118.

WAR DIARY
or
INTELLIGENCE SUMMARY.   213 Machine Gun Company
(Erase heading not required.)

Instructions regarding War Diaries and Intelligence Summaries are contained in F.S. Regs., Part II. and the Staff Manual respectively. Title pages will be prepared in manuscript.

Place	Date	Hour	Summary of Events and Information	Remarks and references to Appendices
MOREUIL	8.10.17		Instructions received that Coy would be relieved by the 9 In Bde on the night of 9/10 inst. Officers of incoming unit made a tour of the line during final emcentrations carried out in conjunction with 28 Bn. Rained nearly all day. Operation Order No. 12 issued	(B) Appx II
MOREUIL	9.10.17		2/Lt GOLSTON to hospital. 2/Lt. T.H.C.O.BOYLE arrived back to Transport lines to carry on of 2nd Coy arrived late for relief. Arrangement re Transport altered on account of Rd on left completely washed. Bus spent relief which was not complete by 12 midnight weather cold and wet	(P)
BEUGNATRE	10.10.17		Relief reported complete by 4.30 am. Bad relief, owing to several impassable entrenancescen arising. Company returned to Camp at BEUGNATRE. Rain during morning fine in afternoon 2/Lt BOYLE visited new Camp.	S.D.
BEUGNATRE	11.10.17		Day spent in cleaning up and packing limbers for move. Coy inspected by Coy Artificer. Weather windy but dry.	S.P.
BEUGNATRE	12.10.17		Company moved to new Camp at BEAULENCOURT. Coy left old Camp on first relieved by 8th 9 Coy. Weather most cold and windy. Trest satisfactory though of course very short. New Camp on 1662 J. Huts Nos & Huts. Bad waggon lines.	R.P.

Norman Capt
Army 213 MGC

Army Form C. 2118.

WAR DIARY
or
INTELLIGENCE SUMMARY.

(Erase heading not required.)

213th Machine Gun Company

Place	Date	Hour	Summary of Events and Information	Remarks and references to Appendices
BEULENCOURT	13.10.17		Day spent in inspection and refitting, cleaning up of Machine Guns	CP
BEULENCOURT	14.10.17		Sunday. Inspection of billets. Divine Service	CP
BEULENCOURT	15.10.17		Training carried out according to programme	CP
BEULENCOURT	16.10.17		Small field firing practice carried out. Weather fine	CP
BEULENCOURT	17.10.17		Training according to programme. Lecture by Arty. Commander	CP
BEULENCOURT	18.10.17		Training according to programme	CP
BEULENCOURT	19.10.17		Training met by Brigadier. Weather fine	CP
BEULENCOURT	20.10.17		Lecture by Lt. Major R.A. Training. Weather fine. Coln. Reconnaissance of battle scheme	CP
BEULENCOURT	21.10.17		Preparation of position for next days Barrage Scheme. Weather fine	CP
BEULENCOURT	22.10.17		Barrage Scheme carried out. Watched by Brig. Gen. 35D.I. and others. Command first attempt not bad. Weather damp. Machine guns returned from exposure	CP
BEULENCOURT	23.10.17		Training as far as weather permitted, it being wet. Also Company matters, outfits	CP
BEULENCOURT	24.10.17		Weather fine. Parade. Lecture by O.C. about Signals. Transport as usual	CP

Noton Capt
O.C. 213 M.G. Coy

Army Form C. 2118.

WAR DIARY
or
INTELLIGENCE SUMMARY.
(Erase heading not required.)

2/3rd Machine Gun Coy

Place	Date	Hour	Summary of Events and Information	Remarks and references to Appendices
BEULENCOURT	25/10/17		Training. Weather unsettled.	Nil
BEULENCOURT	26/10/17		Tactical Scheme. Plan very poorly devised. Weather very wet, result not very satisfactory owing to ignorance of everyone as to ground idea.	Nil
BEULEN COURT	27/10/17		2/Lt Bond back from Course. Weather fine. 3/10 Milhem went on leave.	Nil
BEULEN COURT	28/10/17		Weather fine. Church parade. Brigadier visited Camp	Nil
BEULEN COURT	29/10/17		Lt Miller back from Course. Preparations carried out for moving tomorrow.	Nil
BEULENCOURT	30/10/17		Company moved to GOMIECOURT. Route march carried out satisfactorily. No new fall out. Weather fine but cold during morning but turned wet after arrival.	C/12/13 Nil
GOMIE COURT	31/10/17		Trek continued to MONCHIET where Company was billeted in ADRIAN HUTS, officers in huts. March rather trying owing to route being very hilly but none fell out. Weather beautiful for marching road food. Transport arrived in excellent condition, no trouble of any description being experienced.	Nil App 5 6 7

D Oban Capt
Comdg 2/3 m G Coy

K
213th A G Coy
Appendix No 1.

October 1917.

SECRET   213th Machine Gun Company   COPY No 21
Operation Order No 11

Reference Maps 51ᴮ S.W. 1/10,000   5.10.17
               57ᶜ N.W. 1/10,000

1. The 213th M.G. Coy will relieve 12 guns of the 208th M.G. Coy & 4 guns of the 212th M.G. Coy on the night of the 6/7th inst.

2. The relief will be carried out in accordance with attached table.

3. For purposes of control the grouping of guns is as follows:

Guns	Group	Group Commander	Group H.Q.
18, 19	APEX	2/Lt. J. McFARLANE	Pudsey Support with H.Q. of Inf Coy. holding APEX
22(1), 22(2), 24, 25	RAILWAY	2/Lt. C.J. EASTON	RAILWAY CUTTING
20, 21(1), 21(2)	HALIFAX	2/Lt. A.W. SPENCER	HOBART CROSS
20 A, 16, 23 A, 25 A, 26 A, 27 A, 28 A(?)	INTERMEDIATE	2/Lt. A.K. STIRLING	COY. H.Q

4. At each position
    Trench Stores
    Tripods
    Belt Boxes

will be taken over. A list showing material taken over will be forwarded to Coy HQ by 12 noon 7.10.17.

(2)

5. The greatest care must be exercised in order to ensure that Standing & Tactical Orders are taken over & properly understood. The Group Commander will personally check the tactical orders of all his guns & will render a certificate to Coy H.Q. by 6 pm on the 7.10.17 stating that he has done so.

Explicit information regarding work in hand must also be obtained.

6. One limber (referred to in Table of Relief as L.1) will go to the junction of RAILWAY RESERVE & TANK AVENUE. This limber will drop its rear portion at G.9.b.00.65 & pick it up again on its way out.

One limber (referred to in Table of Relief as L.2) will go to the Railway ration dump. This limber will drop its rear portion at 1CAREE CORNER & pick it up again on its way out.

One half limber (referred to in Table of Relief as L.3) will go to HOBART CROSS.

    L 1 will bring out 1 gun of 205 Coy & 4 of 212 Coy
    L 2 " " " 7 guns " 208 "
    L 3 " " " 4 " " 208 "

Two limbers will be required for H.Q.

7. Relief will be reported to Coy H.Q. by the word "ENCORE ——— p m" the message being sent in the group commander's name.

8. ACKNOWLEDGE.

Issued by hand at 8.15 pm.

L. Shaw
Capt
Cmdg 213th M.G. Coy.

SECRET

Table of Relief

No of Gun	Location of Gun	Group	(recorded by)	Wind by	Ranging rounds of shells	Times of meeting guns	
18	65 b 9.5.	APEX	208	C. Section	Railway Pt.6	8.15 hrs	L 2 (Fore)
19	65 a 05.95	"	208	C	Junction of Railway near Stankirk	"	L 1 (Fore)
22(1)	65 d 85.75.	RAILWAY	208	B	Railway Station Pump	"	L 2 (Fore)
22(2)	65 d 30.65	"	208	B	"	"	L 2 (Fore)
24	65 a 3.3	"	208	B	"	"	L 2 (Fore)
25	64 t 80.55	"	212	B	Junction of Railway Reserve & Stankirk	"	L 1 (Fore)
20	61 t 15.15.	HALIFAX	208	a	Hobart Cross	"	L 3
21(1)	61 t 25.65	"	208	a	"	"	L 3
21(2)	61 d 45.35	"	208	a	"	"	L 3
20 A	61 c 85.65	INTERMEDIATE	208	D	Ogance Corner	8.0 hrs	L 2 (Rear)
16	61 a 75.05	"	208	D	"	"	L 2 (Rear)
23 A	61 a 7.1	"	208	D	"	"	L 2 (Rear)
25 A	61 a 45.65.	"	208	D	"	"	L 2 (Rear)
26 A	69 f 5.5	"	212	a	C9 t 00.65	"	L 1 (Rear)
27 A	69 b 10.45	"	212	C	"	"	L 2 (Rear)
28 A(1)	63 c 40.15	"	212	C	"	"	L 1 (Rear)

213th M.G. Coy
Appendix No 2

October 1917.

SECRET   213th M. G. Coy   COPY No 2
                   Operation Order No 12.

Reference maps 51ᴮ S.W. 1/10,000   8.10.17.
               57ᶜ N.W. 1/10,000

1. The 213th M. G. Coy will be relieved by the 9th M.G. Coy on the night of the 9th/10th inst.

2. Relief will be carried out in accordance with attached table.

3. Each guide will be in possession of a slip of paper stating from which position he comes.

4. At each position
        10 belt boxes
        1 petrol can
        Trench stores
will be handed over but nothing else.
List of material handed over will be prepared in duplicate. One copy will be handed to the incoming teams & the other which must be receipted will be retained & forwarded to Coy H.Q. by 12 noon on the 10.10.17.

5. All positions, dugouts & latrines must be handed over in a tidy & sanitary condition, & a certificate stating that this has been done & signed by the incoming teams will be forwarded to Coy H.Q. by 12 noon on 10.10.17.

6. All information regarding the gun positions must be handed over with the utmost care. Gun commanders will hand over Standing & Tactical orders, at the same time explaining the latter to the incoming gun commanders. Group commanders will prepare statements regarding the tactical duties of their guns & all pertinent information

Full details regarding work on hand will also be explained. All maps & barrage tables dealing with the sector will be handed over.

7. On completion of relief, gun teams will return independently to camp.

8. The following transport will be required:—
One limber (L.1) to report at the Junction of RAILWAY RESERVE & TANK AVENUE at 7.30 p.m. This limber on its way up will drop its rear portion at C9 b 02.65. & pick it up again on its way out.
One limber (L.2) to report at the RAILWAY RATION DUMP at 7.30 p.m. This limber on its way up will drop its rear portion at IDAREE CORNER & pick it up again on its way out.
One half limber will report at HOBART CROSS at 7.30 p.m.
Two limbers will report at COY. H.Q. at 7.30 p.m.

9. Relief will be reported to COY. H.Q by the word "ENFIN _____ p.m.", the message being sent in the Group Commanders name.

10. ACKNOWLEDGE.

Issued by hand at 9.30 p.m.

L. Phare Capt.
Cmdg 213th M. G. Coy.

Copies to.
1. ~~~~
2/3 War Diary
4. ~~~~~~~~~~
5. ~~~~~~~~~~
6. " D. Millikin
7. " C. T. Easton
8. " a. W. Spencer
9. " a. Stirling
10. " A. T. Gulston
11. C. S. M.
12. C. Q. M. S.
13. 9th M. G. Coy

SECRET

Table of Relief

No. of Gun Group	Location of Gun	Group	Rendezvous of Guides	Times of meeting Guides	Outgoing Track for emergency Rendezvous	Rendezvous
18	C.5.d.9.5	APEX	RLY. RATION DUMP	7.30 a.m.	L 2 (Fore)	RLY. RATION DUMP
19	U.29.a.03.95	"	"	"	L 1 (Fore)	JUNCTION OF RLY RESERVE & TANK AVE
22(1)	C.5.d.55.75	RAILWAY	"	"	L 2 (Fore)	RLY. RATION DUMP
22(2)	C.5.d.30.85	"	"	"	"	"
24	C.5.a.3.3	"	"	"	"	"
25	C.4.b.80.55	"	"	"	L 1 (Fore)	JUNCTION OF RLY RESERVE & TANK AVE
20	C.11.b.15.15	HOBART	HOBART. CROSS.	7.15 p.m.	L 3	HOBART CROSS
21(1)	C.11.b.25.65	"	"	"	"	"
21(2)	C.5.d.45.35	"	"	"	"	"
20A	C.10.c.85.65	IGAREE	IGAREE CORNER	7 p.m.	L 2 (Rear)	IGAREE CORNER
16	C.10.a.75.05	"	"	"	"	"
23A	C.10.a.7.1.	"	"	"	"	"
25A	C.10.a.45.65	"	"	"	"	"
26A	C.9.b.5.5	H.Q.	COY H.Q.	"	L 1 (Rear)	C.9.b.00.65
27A	C.9.b.10.75	"	"	"	"	"
28A(1)	C.3.c.40.15	"	"	"	"	"

213 M.G. Coy

Appendix No 3

October 1917

SECRET   213th Machine Gun Company   Copy No 2
              Operation Order No 13

Reference map LENS 1/100,000   29.10.17

1. On the 30th inst the company will march to the COMIECOURT – COURCELLES. AREA.
   The march will be resumed on the 31st inst to the GOUY – SIMENCOURT. AREA.

2. Full marching order and steel helmets will be worn the greatest attention will be paid to smartness of appearance & fitting of equipment. The sections will march in front of the transport. Attention is directed to Company Routine Order No 30 dated 13.10.17.

3. The blankets of each section, including the transport will be carried on their own limbers, the blankets of the transport will be made into a separate roll. Blankets will be rolled up in tens, & all rolls must be labelled. All blankets will be packed on limbers by 1.30am. All other blankets will be carried on the lorry.

4. Section officers kits will be carried on their limbers, on which they must be packed by 7.a.m.

5. One lorry has been allotted to this company for stores. One man will be detailed to report at 6.50am. to a Staff Officer, at the Y.M.C.A. hut BEAUMENCOURT to act as guide.

6. 1 N.C.O. & 4 men will be detailed, from the section on duty, to remain behind & hand over camp. The N.C.O. i/c of this party will obtain a certificate of cleanliness of the camp & a receipt for tentage & stores from the Area Commandant. This certificate and

[P.T.O.

receipt, which in each case must be obtained in duplicate, will be handed in to Coy. H.Q. upon arrival at GOMIECOURT.

7. The Company will parade at 7.45 a.m. Section Commanders will inspect their sections prior to the Company parade.

8. ACKNOWLEDGE

Issued by hand 9.25 p.

~~1. Adj~~
2/3. War diary
~~4. Lt. SPENCER~~
5. " E.W. DENT.
6. " C.J. EASTON.
7. Lt. R.F.C. OXLEY BOYLE.
8. 2Lt. A.R. STIRLING
9. " A.S. OULSTON
10. C.S.M.
11. C.Q.M.S.
~~12. 186th INF. BDE~~

L.P. Khan Capt
Cmdg 213th M.G. Coy

213 MG Coy
Appendix No 4

October 1917

War Diary

213th Machine Gun Company

Training Programme Oct 15th to Oct 20th 1917

Date	8.30 – 9.30	9.30 – 10.30	10.30 – 11.30	11.30 – 12.30	2 – 3	3 – 4	Remarks
Oct 15	Infantry drill	Immediate action	Elevation (elementary)	Fire direction methods of distinguishing and elevation	Rifle and revolver shooting	Judging distance and Range cards	
Oct 16	Rehearsal and adjustments	Fire direction (Practice laying guns)		Immediate action	Bombing	Visual training (Indication and Recognition of targets)	
Oct 17	Infantry drill	Immediate action (rough ground)		Fire direction (practically on given types of ground)			
Oct 18	Infantry drill	Immediate action		Rifle and revolver shooting			
Oct 19	Range						Night operations (2 hours)
Oct 20	Infantry drill	Action (trenches)	Fire direction (Practice fire orders)		Booking		

R. Ney Boyle Lt Capt.
Cmdg 213th M.G. Coy

213 Wm G Coy

Appendix No 5

October 1917

War Diary

Copy No 2

Company Routine Orders
 by Capt L. A. Pollak.
 cmdg. 213th M. G. Coy

1st Oct. 1917.

No 10. Steel Helmets.
 The steel helmet will invariably be worn at training & by guards.

No 11. Anti-Aircraft Mounting
 Whenever the Mark IV tripod is used with reversed cross-head as an A.A. mounting, the direction dial must be removed. Failure to do so, results in serious damage being done to the dial.

No 12. Issue of Clothing & Gun Material.
 Section Officers will always attend whenever any clothing or gun material is being issued to their Sections. The Q.M.S. will under no circumstances issue clothing or gun material except in the presence of an Officer. All clothing & gun material issued from the Q.M. stores will be signed for by the Section Officer in the book allotted for the purpose.

No 13 Broken & damaged Articles of Equipment.
 It must be impressed upon all ranks the absolute necessity of returning to the Q.M. stores, all broken parts of equipment & gun material. A new article can be obtained when the broken portions are produced, but when this is not done the article will have to be paid for by the soldier responsible.

No 14. Smoking in the Horse Lines.
 It has been noticed that some men are in the habit of smoking whilst grooming or carrying out other duties in the horse lines.

This practice will cease at once, no smoking being permitted at any time in the horse lines or in the neighbourhood of the forage shed.

No 15. Designation of Sections.

The Sections will be known as A, B, C & D, in place of the existing appellation of 1, 2, 3 & 4. This designation will be taken into use forthwith.

No 16. Duties of Guards.

Extracts from paras. 1800 & 1801, King's Regulations are re-published for information & future guidance.

Para. 1800:— To Regimental C.O's irrespective of their army rank — their regimental guards are to turn out, & present arms once a day.

Para. 1801:— When a general officer in uniform, or a person entitled to a salute, passes in rear of a guard, the commander is to cause his guard to fall in & stand with sloped arms, facing the front. When such officers pass guards while in the act of relieving, both guards are to salute as they stand, receiving the word of command from the senior commander.

No 17. Blankets – Infection.

All patients admitted to Field Ambulances whose cases have been diagnosed by Regimental Medical Officers as "Trench Fever" or P.U.O. are to be considered as infectious, & will take their blankets with them. These blankets will be disinfected under Field Ambulance arrangements, & handed over to D.A.D.O.S. weekly, from whom they can be obtained on application by the units concerned.

Officers Commanding Field Ambulances will send to D.A.D.O.S. on Sunday mornings a list, showing by units, the number of blankets received during the previous week.

No 18. Iron Ration Tins

As many empty ration tins as possible are to be sent to Base. They should be done up in sacks & returned through Units Supply Officer.

No 19. Leakage of Information.

It is forbidden, except in the course of duty, to discuss or refer to any movement of troops, or to the situation of any body of troops, or to operations of any kind whatsoever.

Where evidence is forthcoming that any Officer, Warrant Officer, Non-commissioned Officer or Private Soldier has disobeyed this Order, he will be tried by Court-martial.

No 20. Censorship.

The attention of all ranks is to be drawn to the second & third paragraphs of the prefix to Censorship Orders, Extracts from G.R.O., Part 1, dated 1.7.17, page 43.

It should be impressed upon all ranks that letters carried on the persons of soldiers going into the front line constitute a grave danger to the secrecy which is necessary for success in military operations.

The following orders issued by German Army Commanders, dated 25th July, show the information which the enemy has obtained from letters:-

"It is again brought to notice that, apart from the statements of prisoners, our most valuable information comes from letters & documents found on them."

"The recent doubts which have existed as to the participation of French troops in the English offensive (in Flanders) have been removed by this letter emanating from a private soldier."

No. 21. Waterproof Sheets – Salvage.

On account of the shortage of rubber, care is to be taken to salve all waterproof sheets possible & other articles containing rubber.

No. 22. Revolvers.

All ranks having revolvers or other pistols, whether public or private property, are forbidden to keep them loaded at times other than when they are in trenches or when firing at pistol practice.

No revolver or other pistol is to be cleaned, outside or inside, while there is a cartridge either in the drum, magazine or chamber. A plea of ignorance of cartridges being in any part of a revolver or pistol while being cleaned will not be accepted as an excuse for non-compliance with this order.

L. Pollack Capt.
cmdg 213th M.G. Coy.

Copy No. 2

Company Routine Orders
by Capt L. A. Pollak,
cmdg 213th M. G. Coy.

7th Oct. 1917

No. 23. Cutting of Wood.

Damage has been caused to Woods & Forests in the Third Army area by the indiscriminate cutting of wood by Units & individuals, without reference either to the owners or higher authority.

Wood can only be cut after the necessary arrangements have been made with the owners by the Forest Control Officer, Third Army.

All applications to cut wood for fuel will be referred through the Corps & Divisional Hdqtrs for Corps & Divisional Troops.

Applications to cut wood for engineer purposes will be referred through C.R.E's & C.E's to the Forest Control Officer, Third Army.

It is forbidden to cut wood in the Third Army Area until application has been made & sanction received, as above.

No. 24. Applications for back pay.

All men wishing to draw back pay that may be due to them must make application in writing, stating the amount required & at the same time forwarding their pay-books for examination.

No. 25. Identity Discs.

Identity discs are not, in future, to be worn next the person. They are to be worn outside the shirt, with the cord round the neck. They are to be worn in no other position. Care must be taken when stamping the discs that the marking is clear & effective.

No 26. Courses of Instruction

All Officers, Officer's servants, N.C.O's & men detailed to attend courses of instruction outside the Division, will be relieved from the trenches 48 hours before they are due to start on their journey. They will proceed to their transport lines.

Quartermaster will be responsible for seeing that each N.C.O, man, & servant proceeds equipped as stated below:—

Fully armed & equipped.
Clothing in a state fit to stand 6 weeks hard wear.
Two complete sets of underclothing.
Three pairs of socks.
Smoke helmet & box respirators.
Wire breakers (N.C.O's only) (Army Schools only.)
Complete necessaries.
Blanket.
Steel helmet.
Ground sheet.
Paid for a fortnight from commencement of course
Rationed for day after arrival (if ordered)
Have bathed & clothing disinfected.
Are in a fit state of health to proceed.

Transport Officer will be responsible that N.C.O's & men are properly equipped & will personally inspect them prior to their departure.

D. M. Mullikin 2/Lt.
for Capt.
Cmdg 213th M.G.C.

Company Routine Orders   Copy No. 2
    by Capt. K. A. Pollok
Cmdg 213th M. G. Coy

15 Oct 1917

No 27. Riding on Limbers

All ranks are absolutely forbidden from riding on limbered waggons. In the event of a man becoming ill & it being impossible to obtain the necessary transport to move him, an Officer may give a man permission to ride on a limber.

This permission which must be given very sparingly, will be given to the soldier in writing.

Any breach of this order will be severely dealt with.

No 28. Limber Covers

Covers will invariably be kept on limbers when standing on the waggon lines & whenever possible when the limbers are in use. Care must be taken that the covers are properly secured, all the cords being tied, & the corner straps buckled.

No 29. Falling out on the march

No man will under any circumstances whatsoever fall out without permission when on the march. In the event of a soldier feeling unable to proceed further on account of illness, he will apply to his Section Officer, who will give permission in writing, at the same time detailing a N.C.O to bring him along as quickly as possible.

No 30. Brakesmen

Whenever the Coy moves with its transport brakesman must be detailed for each limber.

Section Cmdrs are responsible that men are detailed for this duty.

Whenever the entire Coy is out for a route

march or trek, brakesmen will be detailed as follows

Fighting limbers.	Section Corporals
S.A.A. limbers.	Section Officers batmen
N'dqk limber.	C.O's batman.
Water cart.	Watermen.
Cooks cart.	Artificer.

No 31. Anti fire precautions

Two tins or buckets will be allotted to each hut one of which will be filled with water & one with sand.

Under no circumstances whatsoever will these buckets be removed except for the purpose of extinguishing a fire. The sanitary fatigue are responsible that the buckets are in position & full.

No 32. Limber Corporals

Unless orders are issued to the contrary, whenever the Coy goes into the line, each Section will detail one of its Corporals to remain behind at the waggon lines to act as Limber Corporal.

The duties of these Cpls is to look after the section limbers, gun material, & kit which is not taken into the trenches. They will also come up with the ration transport each night & will be responsible for the proper distribution of the rations to their respective gun teams.

The attention of these Cpls is directed to Coy Routine Order No 27 published today.

No 33. Bricks

No bricks are to be taken from the Brick Yard in P.21.d. without reference to Corps H'dqtrs.

R Delysayle Lt Capt
Cmdg 213 M. G. Coy

War Diary.

Company Routine Orders
by Capt. C. A. Pollak.
Cmdg 213th M. G. Coy.

Copy No. 2

Oct 21/1917

No 34. Alterations of A. B. 64°

When any notification appears in Company Orders Part II affecting the rank or pay of a soldier Section Officers will arrange for the A. B. 64° of the men concerned to be forwarded to the Orderly room with the least possible delay.

It is pointed out that the failure to have the necessary entries made in the book may result in the soldier being unable to draw the pay due to him.

No 35. Braziers.

No braziers allowed in the open after sunset.

No 36. Leaving camp.

Under no circumstances whatsoever are men allowed out of camp unless properly dressed, that is to say, P. H. helmets to be carried and puttees worn.

No 37. Fires.

Army Routine Order No 1183 is published for information and compliance.

To minimise the risk of accidents from fire in hutments, the following orders will be observed:—

(1). All buildings in which stoves are used will be inspected by a responsible officer who will satisfy himself that there is no faulty construction between the flues of stoves and the walls and roof of buildings and will order all defects in this respect to be removed.

[P.T.O

Fires (continued)

(2) Buildings which are readily inflammable, and which, from the nature of their use, are specially liable to catch fire, such as drying rooms or laundries, should be sited at such a distance apart that there shall be no risk of the fire spreading from one building to another.

(3) Where fire hydrants are provided they should be placed not less than 20 ft from the building, otherwise in case of fire, it may not be possible to make use of them.

(4) When stoves are fixed in huts, care is to be taken that no part of the metal flue touches any woodwork. Where the flue passes through a wooden wall or roof it should be cased in with an external pipe, preferably of earthenware, such as a drain pipe. The space between the flue and the outer pipe should be filled with non-inflammable packing. The external pipe should be kept from contact with any wood, the space being covered with some form of metal, e.g., tin biscuit box.

(5) All stoves should stand upon a non-inflammable platform, e.g., brick, stone or concrete.

(6) Some protection should be placed round stoves having open doors or any aperture from which hot cinders can fall on the floor.

(7) Flues must be regularly swept.

(8) A daily inspection of all woodwork near stoves and flues should be made to ascertain that there is no charring of wood in progress.

(9) Fires should be extinguished at "lights out" and the ashes removed outside the hut.

R. Arthur Doyle Lt for Capt
Cmdg 213th M.G. Coy

213th MG Bn.
Appendix No 6

October 1917

203rd Machine Gun Company — No 1
Daily Orders Part II — 10.10.17

1. Promotions and Appointments

63861 L/C Greaves G. — Transport — Appointed unpaid L/C vice 67025 a/L/C Takins deprived of lance stripe 12/9/17 — 12/9/17

68017 L/C Holskamp W. — A. Section — To receive pay of appointment — 9/9/17

2. To Hospital

31706 Pte Treadwell E. — D. Section — Admitted Field Amb — 4/10/17
36338 " Thorne A. — Transport — " " " — 5/10/17
2/Lt A. S. Gulston — " — " " " — 9/10/17

3. From Course

68002 Pte Cryan J. — D. Section — From Infantry Course — 5/10/17

4. From Leave

Lieut R. F. C. Oxley Boyle — D. Section — From leave — 6/10/17

5. Strength Decrease

67773 Pte Hanson H — A. Section — To U.K. sick — 21/9/17
103794 " Bennett C — " — To 45 C.C.S. — 6/10/17

6. To Summer Rest Camp

67761 L/C Gibson B. — B. Section — To S.R.C. — 3/10/17

7. From Summer Rest Camp

54919 Pte Webb B — C. Section — From S.R.C. — 9/10/17
82336 " Ganney J — D " — " " " —

8. **Field Punishment & Deprivation of pay**

103801 Pte Barham W. B. Section — When on active service Neglect of duty whilst on sentry 7/10/17 28 days F.P. No 1 10/10/17

40701 Pte Dixon T. B. " — When on active service Improperly dressed in front line trench 7/10/17 Deprived 10 days pay 10/10/17

68574 Pte Swaddle J. A. " — When on active service neglect of duty whilst on sentry in front line trench 8/10/17 10 days F.P. No 2 10/10/17

N. Cox Capt
Cmdg 213th Tn G.6

213th Machine Gun Company No 2
Daily Orders Part 2   17/10/17

1. Promotions and Appointments.

66604 L/C Kennett E. Appointed A/Cpl vice
                                Cpl Darbyshire promoted 1/9/17

2. Postings.

64401	Pte Condon T.	From B section	to	D Section	17/10/17
27304	" Walker W.	" C	"	" D	"
67997	" Whitehead T.	" C	"	" D	"
106650	" Jones G.	" D	"	" C	"
58899	" O'Donnell A	" D	"	" C	"
15685	" Jackson J	" D	"	" B	"

3. Strength Increase (Rejoined.)

64.232. Pte Chamberlain A. B. Section   Rejoined Coy 11/10/17

4. Strength Decrease (Transfers.)

200064 Pte Davis.A.T.   H.Q Section   Trsfd to 205 M.G.Coy 3/10/17
54034 " Shorthouse D.   "   "   "   "   "   "   12/10/17
                                Authority D.A.A.G.
                                62nd Divn A/17/m/25

5. Punishments.

28385 L/C Jones D   Trspt Section.   W.O.A.S. Absent from
                                    parade 12/10/17. Severely
                                    reprimanded   2/f/of

6. To Hospital.

66665	Pte Littlejohn S	C Section	To hospital	9/10/17
56371	Pte Dale W.	D "	" "	11/10/17
60243	Cpl Reithead R.	D "	" "	16/10/17
103788	Pte Pulteney S	D "	" "	16/10/17
44024	" Davis W.H.	A "	" "	17/10/17

7. From Hospital

58645	Pte Wells H.	D. Section	From hospital	15/10/17
54036	Sgt Darbyshire G.	"	"	do
103042	Pte Gray H.	D	"	17/10/17
31706	" Treadwell C.	D	"	17/10/17

8. Struck off Strength.

103788	Pte Pulteney T. D.	Section	Struck off strength to 2. C.C.S. Depot

9. Promotions and Appointments

51961	Pte Hughes A.	A Section	Apptd unpaid L/C v Pte
31150	Pte Newby E. C.	"	Appd L/C and to receive pay of appointment 12/f

10. Correction

68017	L/C Holtkamp W. A.	Section	To receive pay of appointment from 1/6/17 and not as stated in Daily Orders Part 2 No 1. para 1. dated 10/10/17.

Capt
Cmdg 213th M. G. C

War Diary

225th Machine Gun Company
Daily Orders Part II   No 3 (page 1)
24/10/17

1. Promotions and Appointments

66504 A/Cpl Rance A.   D. Section   Promoted Cpl vice   11/9/17
                                       Cpl Darbyshire promoted

9289 A/Cpl McLean C.   C. "   Promoted Cpl to
                                       complete establishment 11/9/17

2. To Hospital

33848 Pte Hurst W.   Trspt "   To hospital   19/10/17
33867 " Boddy C.   "   "   "   "   20/10/17
33881 L/C Greaves G.   "   "   "   "   23/10/17

3. From Hospital

   2/Lt A.S. Gulston   Trspt "   From hospital   22/10/17
66665 Pte Littlefair A. C   "   "   "   22/10/17

4. Officers leave and ration allowance.

   2/Lt J. McFarlane   C. Section   Leave to U.K. 20/10/17 - 30/10/17

5. To Summer rest camp

27767 Pte Austen R.   A. Section   To summer rest camp 20/10/17

6. From Summer rest camp

27761 L/C Gibson D.   B Section   From summer rest camp 20/10/17

7. Inter-section transfer

38488 Sgt Lovett E.   From D. Section to B Section   24/10/17

8 Punishments.

20100 L/C Shepherd J.   C Section   Neglect of duty whilst
                                     on guard 19/10/17.
                                     Reprimanded 19/10/17

(P.T.O.

q. Strength decrease
64415 Pte Edwards. A.E.   H.Q. Section   To U.K. sick 12/10/17
67755 L/C Grimley P   B   "   Arrived Base
                                          Depot   20/10/17
44024 Pte Davis W.H.   A   "   To No 3 C.C.S. 19/10/17
103086 " Mead W   C   "   To No 45 " " 19/10

                                    R. Delly Bayley Lt A/Capt
                              Cmdg 213th M.G. Coy.

War Diary.

213th Machine Gun Company
Daily Orders Part II   No 4 (Page 1)

1. To Hospital
63881 Dr Childs R   Trspt Section   To hospital   23/10/17
67814 Pte Gatland G   B   "   "   29/10/17

2. From Hospital
63861 L/C Greaves G   Trspt   "   From hospital   26/10/17
64238 Pte Brown J.J   D   "   "   "   29/10/17

3. To Course
63888 Dr Garrod C   Trspt   "   To course   1/11/17

4. From Course
2/Lt C.W Dent   B   "   From course   26/10/17
Lieut R.A.J Miller   HQ   "   "   "   29/10/17
71044 Sgt Handford J.   D   "   "   "   29/10/17
54389 Pte Fox C   B   "   "   "   26/10/17
54478 " Jordan T.   HQ   "   "   "   29/10/17

5. Strength Increase
115755 Pte Wood J.   Joined from Base   29/10/17

6. Strength Decrease
60723 Cpl Geithead D   D   "   To 41 Stationery hospl   28/10/17
63881 Dr Childs R   Trspt   "   " 48 C.C.S.   24/10/17

7. Officers leave & ration allowance
2/Lt D. Millikin   A. Section   Leave to U.K. 29/10/17 – 7/11/17

8. From leave
2/Lt J. McFarlane   C   "   From leave   1/11/17

9. From Summer Rest Camp
67764 Pte Austin R   A   "   From S.R.C.   30/10/17

10. Postings
115755 Pte Wood J.   Posted to B. Section   29/10/17

R.A.J Miller fo. Capt.
Cmdg 213th M.G. Coy

213th M G Cny
Appendix No 4

October 1917

Company orders by
Capt P. A. Pollak
Cmdg 213th M.G. Coy

Oct 30/1917

Reveille 6 AM
Breakfast 7 "
Dinner on arrival of Coy in new camp

The Coy will move tomorrow to MONCHIET.

The Coy will march in the same order & dress as today.

Blankets will be packed on limbers by 7 AM, officer kits by 7.30 AM.

Tomorrow's dinner ration will be issued out by the C.Q.M.S. to limber brakesmen. These will be placed on the limber & brakesman will be responsible that these rations are returned intact to C.S.M. on arrival at new camp. All dixies will be carried on the limbers.

One lorry is allotted to this Coy for stores. This lorry will make one journey first for the T.M.B. Pte Bracey will report to the T.M.B. at 7.30 AM tomorrow, when he will proceed with this lorry on its first journey & then guide it back to the Coy dump.

A rear party of 1 N.C.O. & 6 men will be detailed from the section on duty to clean up the camp & to load the lorry on its return. This party will then be marched by the N.C.O. in charge to the new camp, reporting their arrival at Coy H.Q.

The attention of all ranks is directed to the points mentioned today regarding wearing of equipment. The strictest march discipline will be maintained.

The Coy will parade at 8.45 AM.

Lieut R.A. Miller
" R.F.C. Oxley Boyle
2/Lt E.W. Dent
a.s. Gulston
" G.F. Stirling

C.S.M.
C.Q.M.S.
H.S. Orderly Sgt.

Capt
Cmdg 213th M.G. Coy

213 M.W.Coy
Appendix No 7

Oct 1917

Original

SECRET

Vol 9

War Diary
of
213th Machine Gun Coy

From 1/7/17 To 30/11/17

Volume No. 9

Officer i/c
Cmdg 213 K.M.G Coy

Army Form C. 2118.

WAR DIARY
or
INTELLIGENCE SUMMARY.
(Erase heading not required.)

2/3 Coy. M.G.C.

Place	Date	Hour	Summary of Events and Information	Remarks and references to Appendices
MONCHIET	1-11-17	12 Noon	General clean up of Coy & washing limbers. 2nd Lt McFarlane returned from leave to U.K.	D.H.W.
	2-11-17	"	Coy training. Weather fine.	D.H.W.
	3-11-17	"	Coy Training. 5 O.R's from each Battalion reported to this unit & were attached as carrying party.	D.H.W.
	4-11-17	"	Church Parade. Brigadier General G.F. HILL inspected attached infantry.	D.H.W.
	5-11-17	"	Coy Training. Weather fine.	D.H.W.
	6-11-17	"	Range Practice. Baths for Coy in afternoon, weather wet.	D.H.W.
	7-11-17	"	Tank Demonstration at WAILLY. Steady Rain.	D.H.W.
	8-11-17	"	Coy Training in Box & drill. Weather fine.	D.H.W.
	9-11-17	"	Route march. Weather wet.	D.H.W. APPENDIX I
	10-11-17	"	2nd Lt Millikin rejoined unit from leave to U.K. 2/Cpl Collins embarked for U.K. Report to Cadet Unit. Conference at Bde H.Q.	D.H.W.
	11-11-17	"	Church Parade. 12 Occasional Training.	D.H.W.
	12-11-17	"	Capt Pollock went forward to new area with G.S.O.I. Brig. Gen. BRADFORD. V.C. inspected Coy. Preparing for move. Conference at Bde H.Q.	D.H.W.
	13-11-17	12 Noon	Packing limbers & cleaning up camp preparatory to move in the evening. 6:30 P.M. Coy started to march to MONCHIET - LE PETIT arriving in billets there at 12:15 A.M. No mad casualties.	D.H.W. APPENDIX II

WAR DIARY or INTELLIGENCE SUMMARY

Army Form C. 2118.

213 M.G. Coy

Place	Date	Hour	Summary of Events and Information	Remarks and references to Appendices
ACHIET LE PETIT	14-11-17	12 Noon	Coy in tents at Achiet-le-petit. Coy preparing for impending operations.	Appx III
	15-11-17	"	Coy preparing for impending operations & fitting clothing.	Appx III
	16-11-17	"	Church Parade at 12.15 P.M. O6 Conference at Bde H.Q. at 11.30 A.M. Coy preparing for move to LECHELLE. Coy marched starting point at 5 P.M. & arrived in Billets at LECHELLE 1.55 A.M. 17th inst.	APPENDIX 3 Appx III
LECHELLE	17-11-17	"	Coy drew 160,000 rds S.A.A. from IV Corps dump on the night of Oct 17th a Coy S.A.A. dump of 160,000 rds was formed at in the vicinity of BUTLERS CROSS. HAVRINCOURT WOOD. 16 Barrage position were also prepared in vicinity of Butlers Cross.	Appx III
	18-11-17	"	Coy moved to M.G. Camp at BERTINCOURT at 4.20 P.M.	Appx III
	19-11-17	"	C.O.s Conference at H.Q. 2/4 Bn. D.of W. Regt. at 11.30. Coy moved up to Barrage positions at Butlers Cross about 3.30 P.M. Mens packs & Blankets dumped at Bde Dump. BERTINCOURT. at 4 P.M. Coy moved into the line in the HAVRINCOURT sector & took up a battery position in the neighbourhood of BUTLERS CROSS 70 B 22. Battery was in position about 11 P.M. South bombardment about 5 a.m. which caused the Coys 5 casualties 3 killed & 2 wounded. One fairly heavy south put out of action at 6 a.m. C.O. proceeded to Bde H.Q. at PLACE MORE M1 at 2100 hour 5 20 19 gun put out of action at 6 a.m. Battn only opened fire about zero plus 10 owing to attacking infantry masking fire for the 1st 10 mins.	Appx III
HAVRINCOURT WOOD	20/11/17	"	At 8.45 a.m. 186 Bde (Reserve Bde) was ordered to advance Battn loaded up on pak mules & moved as follows. 2nd Lt. Burton 3 D section under 2nd Lt ORLEY BOYLE & 4th D.o.W. Lt Boston of A section under 2nd Lt. Spencer 2/6 D.o.W. 2 S.6 section of A section under Sgt CAMPBELL with 2/7 D.o.W. & C section 1 of section of B section under 2nd Lt McFARLANE moved forward independently to battery points to assist advance of 2/4 D.o.W. on GRAINCOURT 2d & section of D section 4 one gun of D section under 2nd Lt MILLIKIN moved at 10.00 a.m. to HAVRINCOURT & took up defensive position in trenches about N 23 d. Recon N.E. of Hindenburg Support as FLESQUIERES was M.G. opposed other D.o.W. were unable to proceed further.	Appx 3

WAR DIARY or INTELLIGENCE SUMMARY

Army Form C. 2118.

213 M.G. Coy

Place	Date	Hour	Summary of Events and Information	Remarks and references to Appendices
HAVRINCOURT	21/11/17		Nos. 2, 3, C & D moved to company from FLESQUIERES other sub sections moved with Battalions to which they were attached. Lt Boyle's Sub section being at GRAINCOURT Sgt CAMPBELL'S sub section being at E 28 b.3, 2nd Lt. SPENCER'S subsection being at KANGAROO ALLEY about E 28 C.0.0. Coy HQ at BERTINCOURT. 2nd Lt. McFARLANE'S battery moved to GRAINCOURT at 10 AM 2/4 Dorset Regt advance at dawn. 2nd Lt. McFARLANE formed ANNEX the advance was supported by men of the farm at GRAINCOURT under K.G.C. C Section under 2nd Lt. McFARLANE Boyle's subsection which is about nineteen road. Covering with the Battalion & after capturing the village took up chosen positions with advanced with the Battalion & after capturing the village. Crowelth in attack 2 O.R.s wounded. Two guns on either flank of the village Crowelth under 2nd Lt. McFARLANE proceeded under 2nd Lt. A released. B section originally under 2nd Lt. McFARLANE, proceeded under 2nd Lt. EASTON adjusted to O.C. 2/7 B.D. of W. Regt in the factory at E 29 A & placed two 186 Bde guns in the trench WEST of FACTORY. E 23 C. B.Coy was relieved that night & guns withdrawn on relief being complete; arriving at Cover of Lentil Battery Position in K 10 C 2.4. remained in reserve. Rear Coy HQ still at BERTINCOURT.	RMcW
	22-11-17		Guns & elements in reserve until evening when the Div was relieved in the line by the 40th Div. When the Coy started to withdraw to HAVRINCOURT WOOD owing to the delays a state of uncertainty after men this move was not complete that night.	RMcW
	23-11-17		Withdrawal was continued & completed by about 1 P.M. When the Coy returned to its camp at BERTINCOURT G.O.C. tanks camp & congratulated the Coy with manner in which it carried out the tasks allotted to it remainder of day spent resting.	RMcW
BERTINCOURT	24-11-17		Abt 12 noon orders were received for Bgde also to stand by ready to move at 2 hours notice this was reduced to 1 hour notice at 5 P.M.	RMcW

WAR DIARY or INTELLIGENCE SUMMARY

Army Form C. 2118.

213 Coy M.G.C.

Place	Date	Hour	Summary of Events and Information	Remarks and references to Appendices
BERTINCOURT	25-11-17		Orders were received that 62nd Div would relieve 40th Div in the line that night. Coy moved at 2 P.M. & marched via HERMIES. Disposition of Coy as follows. A subsection of D section under 2nd Lt DENT attached 2nd/Lt MILIKIN attached to 2/7 Bn D of W Regt. 2 a subsection of B section under 2nd/Lt Boyle about 119 M.G. Coy remaining 6 guns in 2 subsections of D section under 2nd/Lt Boyle relieved 119 M.G. Coy about F.14.C. Survey at Coy H.Q. at F.19.b.19 Relief complete about 11 P.M. Coy vicinity Bde H.Q. at CATACOMBS.	MMW
F14 C	26-11-17		QUARINCOURT where instructions Re deployment of Bde front & orders for attack the next day were received. At about 8pm 2nd Lt Boyle withdrew his guns to Coy H.Q. by Bde H.Q. leaving 1 gun put out of action 1 man killed 2 others shell shock at Stand of Too Coy H.Q. Instructions for attack as follows. Reorganisation of D section under 2nd/Lt MILIKIN Distribution of guns as follows. 2nd Lt DENT attached 2/6 Bn D of W Regt attached to 2/7 Bn D. of W. Regt a subsection under 2nd/Lt MCFARLANE attached 2/6 Bn D. of W. Regt 2/4 Bn D of W Regt one gun of B section, 1 gun Je section under Sgt. FULFORD attached 2/4 Bn D of W Regt C 2nd Lt 1 gun Dent 2 guns under C.O. Rest aiming guns compos.of. A sect 2 guns along road running NW to IMBRUCHEUF to follow attack and take up position not being taken guns were placed S.E. in F.7.a.9.6 owing to all objectives not being taken approx F.7.C. 3.6. STAR CROSS ROADS. F.7.D.3.4. along line in BOURLON WOOD running approx F.7c.3.6. 1 gun C section 2nd Lt MC 1.7.D.4.3. This battery was ultimately formed by (A) 1 gun torn Dent under 2nd/Lt MILIKIN FARLANE the others having been knocked out. (B) 1 gun torn Dent torn knocked out with this system by the gun having been disabled. 2nd/Lt MILIKIN had lost touch with his other gun which had advanced with this system Coy (C) 1 gun Bracken under 2nd/Lt DENT. the other gun of this subsection was put out of action.	MMW
F14 C	27-11-17			

Army Form C.-2118.

213 Coy
M.G.C.

WAR DIARY
or
INTELLIGENCE SUMMARY.
(Erase heading not required.)

Place	Date	Hour	Summary of Events and Information	Remarks and references to Appendices
F.W.C.	27-11-17		All three guns were subjected to heavy shelling throughout the day & the Coy suffered several casualties in addition in sheltering. 2nd Lt MILKIN who was wounded & the subaltern which advanced with the Rnrs suffered casualties especially the subaltern of C section. The C.O. & 2nd Lt McFARLANE carried out a reconnaissance as far as the front in BOURLON VILLAGE where it was ascertained that the tp. had not advanced beyond that point. It was there fore decided to remain in the West but consolidate suffered in that day amounted to will in 30 & 35. The Bde was reinforced that night by a dismounted cavalry Bde (2nd Cav. Div.) the Cavalry took over half nights from the tp by the M.G.Oflrs. Coy remained in position although the line was strengthened by Cavalry Vickers guns. The Bde was relieved that night by 1+21 Bde 2.9 Div. on being Coy withdrew to address Transport lines at K.Q.C. 7.O. Coy was accommodated in tunnel at LOCK. 7. near CANAL.	M.H.W.
F.W.C.	28-11-17		Coy remained at same position until about 4 P.M. when permission was afterwards first to return to the Camp at BERTIN COURT. in arrived at the Camp of Guards M.G.Coy was found in occupation & the Coy was compelled to Bivouac in the Transport field no other billets being available for the men were assessing for Transport to Coy to move next day to LEBUCQUIÈRE	M.H.W.
K.Q.C.7.O.	29-11-17			M.H.W.
LEBUCQUIÈRE	30-11-17		Coy moved according to instruction but on arrival there were orders to report Bde at about X.9 with as little delay as possible. Only 10 guns being in action belts were filled guns packed & Coy moved off at 6 P.M. marching via BEAUMETZ. DOIGNIES. HERMES. & returned to Old location at K.Q.C.7.O.	M.H.W.

WAR DIARY
or
INTELLIGENCE SUMMARY.

213 Coy
M.G.C.

Army Form C. 2118.

Place	Date	Hour	Summary of Events and Information	Remarks and references to Appendices
KQe 7.0.	30-11-17		This morning due to heavy hostile counter attacks which had been followed by small measure of success, the Bde Commander was killed with skull [?]	APPUL APPENDIX 4
			Coy. ROUTINE. ORDERS	APPENDIX 5
			DAILY ORDERS. PART II	

A.S. Miller Lt
Comdg 213 Coy M.G.C.

Appendix
No. 1

213th M.G. Coy.

November 1917

SECRET   213th Machine Gun Company   COPY No.
Operation Order No 14

Reference map. LENS. 11./100.000   13.11.17.

1. On the night of the 13th inst the Company will march to the ACHIET-LE-PETIT. AREA.

2. Full marching order & steel helmets will be worn. The greatest attention will be paid to smartness of appearance & fitting of equipment. Sections will march in front of transport. Attention is directed to Coy Routine Order No 30. dated 15/10/17.

3. Blankets of each section, including transport, will be carried on their own limbers. Blankets of No 1 & 2 gun teams of each Section will be carried on the No 1 limber of that section. No 3 & 4 gun teams on the No 2 limber. Transport blankets on No 3 limber. All limbers will be packed by 12 noon.

4. Section Officers Kits will be carried on their limbers on which they must be packed by 10. AM.

5. Half a lorry has been allotted to the Coy & will carry Quarter-masters stores & artificers tools.

6. One officer 1 N.C.O. & 5. men will be detailed from the section on duty to remain behind & hand over camp. The Officer in charge will obtain a certificate of cleanliness of the camp from the Town Major. All receipts & certificates will be obtained in duplicate. 2/Lt C. J. EASTON will be in charge of this party.

7. Company will parade at 6. 15. p.m.

8. ACKNOWLEDGE.

Issued by hand at 10.30 am.

C. H. Miller. Lieut & Adjt
213th Machine Gun Coy.

1. File
2/3. War Diary.
4. Lt R.H. Oxley-Boyle.
5. 2/Lt J. McFarlane.
6. 2/Lt D. Millikin.
7. " E. W. Dent.
8. " A. S. Gulston
9. " C. J. Easton.
10. " A. K. Stirling.
11. " A. W. Spencer
12. C. S. M.
13. C. Q. M. S.
14. 186th Inf Bde

APPENDIX No 2

213TH M.G. COY.

NOVEMBER 1917

SECRET

To all Officers.

    In view of impending operations, the attached preliminary instructions are forwarded for your information.

    These instructions must be made known to all ranks in your section, but the Commanding Officer relies on the discretion of Section O'mers to impart this information to their men, without arousing suspicion as to coming events.

ACKNOWLEDGE.

                            A. H. Miller Lieut & Adjt.
             Cmdg 213th M.G. Coy.

No. 213 M.G. Coy. Date 10/11/17 R.M 200

SECRET.   COPY No. 3

1. ~~File~~
2/3. War Diary.
~~4. 2/Lt. R.G. Victory Boyle~~
5. 2/Lt. J. McFarlane
6. "   D. Millikin
7. "   E.W. Dent
8. "   A.T. Gulston
9. "   C.J. Easton
10. "   A.K. Stirling
11. "   A.W. Spencer

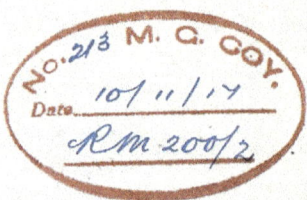

Preliminary Instructions No. 1.

1. Discipline. The word RETIRE does not exist; any man using this word will be shot AT ONCE

2. Trophies Should there be likelihood of captured enemy's guns falling into our hands & it becomes necessary to destroy them, the following action will be taken:-

(a) **Field Guns.** Attack breech mechanism (open) with pick or axe, also the sights & their attachments to the gun or carriage. If time admits, fill the muzzle for a couple of feet or so with earth or any other material, load & fire the gun. As this will burst the gun, it is necessary to fire the gun by a string from a safe place.

(b) **Machine Guns.** Remove lock, feed block & fuzee spring, & bend barrel in front of water jacket with pickaxe.

(c) **Minnenwerfer.** If gun cannot be removed, it should be damaged by denting barrel or blowing up gun if time admits of this.

(d) **Prisoners.** No documents are to be taken from prisoners.

3. Reports. Reports must be correctly written; they are useless unless the following are inserted:-
   1. Locality
   2. Date.
   3. Time of despatch.

N.C.O's must be taught to send in reports. Nil reports must be sent in.

(2)

4. Identifications — It is essential that no orders, maps or correspondence, which, if captured by the enemy would disclose the identity of the Division, should be carried into action.

All ranks taking part in an assault are forbidden to carry any letters, papers, orders or sketches which, in the event of their capture, would be likely to give any information to the enemy.

Officers should not be over burdened with maps; the trench map of the actual area & possibly the local 1/100.000 sheet are all they require for the assault.

5. Runners — Runners should not be sent singly, if it can be avoided, with an important message. A duplicate copy should be sent off a few minutes after the original, & by an alternative route. Runners sent back with demands for stores will remain at the store to guide back the carrying party.

6. White Flag. — No notice is to be taken of a white flag unless the enemy comes out of his trenches unarmed & with hands up

Surrenders. It is the duty of all ranks to continue to use their weapons against the enemy's fighting troops, unless & until it is beyond all doubt that these have not only ceased all resistance, but that, whether through having voluntarily thrown down their weapons or otherwise, they have definitely & finally abandoned all hope or intention of resisting further. In the case of apparent surrender, it lies with the enemy to prove his intention beyond the possibility of misunderstanding before the surrender can be accepted as genuine.

Size of Escorts. These should not exceed 10 per cent. of the prisoners in each batch; no more

(3)

men than are absolutely necessary should be sent back from the front line; carrying parties returning for more stores & slightly wounded walking cases should be used where possible

7. **Wounded men** No unwounded man is to fall out to help a wounded man back.

Slight Wounds. Officers & men who are wounded in the course of the operations, but whose wounds do not wholly incapacitate them, should continue to take an active part in the fight until ordered to the rear by a superior officer.

The presence of a wounded officer, N.C.O, or man in the ranks, who, though wounded, has the grit to continue fighting, is a fine example of courage & most inspiring to his comrades.

Discarding of Arms & Equipment. Wounded men must not be allowed to discard their arms & equipment, unless their wounds are so severe as to render the men incapable of carrying them.

The soldier must be taught that it is a point of honour to carry his arms as long as he possibly can. Lightly wounded walking cases, who have disobeyed this order, should be sent back by the Trench Police to fetch their rifles & equipment.

8. **Collection of Trophies** There is to be no collecting of trophies and souvenirs. & Men found hunting for them will be most severely dealt with.

9. **Water** There should be one day's supply in the mens waterbottles, & Section Cmdrs should ensure that the waterbottles are filled. Water must be used most sparingly. No food or water found in German trenches is to be eaten or drunk until it has been examined & passed fit by a Medical Officer.

(4)

10. Carrying Parties Carrying or working parties should not be allowed to come back empty handed from the front; every man should be put on his honour to bring back something. This does not refer to the collection of useless souvenirs, but to articles of military value. The collection of rifles is of the utmost importance. Empty ration limbers or mules returning from the front should be used to carry back salvage to Brigade & Divisional Dumps.

11. Action during Attack Directly a position is taken, consolidation will be carried out without delay. Under no circumstances must men be allowed to sit down & rest until the position has been placed in a proper state of defence.

12. Rations. The "iron ration" & the unexpended portion of the days ration will always be carried

13. Ammunition Every N.C.O. & man without exception will carry 2 bandoliers of 50 rounds each.

14. Enemy Ruses. The enemy carry their machine guns in a sledge & sometimes throw a blanket over the gun. At a distance this makes the sledge & gun resemble a stretcher. Enemy stretcher bearers should therefore be treated with suspicion

15. Orders Reports & Messages The attention of all officers is directed to the general instructions regarding the preparation & despatch of orders, reports & messages, as described in "Field Service Pocket Book" Chapter 3 Section 12.

APPENDIX.
No 3

213TH M. G. Coy.

NOVEMBER 1917

SECRET. 213th Machine Gun Company   COPY No. 2
            Preliminary Scheme
Reference map 57c N.E.4 1/10,000
            57c N.E.3 1/10,000   16/11/17
            MOEUVRES 1/20,000

The operations are divided into 2 phases.
  (A) Action during attack by 185th & 187th Brigades
  (B) Action during attack by 186th Brigade

<u>A</u> (1) The Company will be divided into 2 eight gun batteries
(2)(a) <u>Right Battery.</u>
    <u>Battery Commander.</u>   2/LT. J. McFARLANE.
    <u>Composition of Battery</u>
       B Section   2/LT. E.W. DENT.
       C   "   2/LT C.J. EASTON.
    <u>Location of Battery</u> about Q 4 d 2.4
    <u>Objective of Battery</u> outskirts of HAVRINCOURT VILLAGE
from K 28 c 35.65., K 28 c 6.7., K 28 a 50.55., K 28 a 75.65.,
K 28 a 65.70., thence along road to K 22 d 15.30.
thence along railway to K 23 a 45.15
    <u>Periods of Fire</u>   to be issued later
    <u>S.A.A. Dump</u>   Cross roads Q 4 d. 2.0.
(b) <u>Left Battery.</u>
    <u>Battery Commander.</u>   LIEUT. R.F.C. OXLEY-BOYLE.
    <u>Composition of Battery</u>
       A Section   2/LT A.W. SPENCER.
       D   "   2/LT. D. MILLIKIN.
    <u>Location of Battery</u> about Q 3 b 4.2.
    <u>Objective of Battery</u> K 27 d 50.45. to K 28 c 35.65.
    then lift to   K 27 b 3.3. to K 28 a 50.55.
    then lift again to   K 21 d 4.2 to K 22 c. 55.30
    <u>Periods of Fire</u>   to be notified later
    <u>S.A.A. Dump</u>   Q.3.b.2.2. (BUTLERS CROSS)

(3) Immediately on cessation of barrage fire, all guns will be packed ready to move and sections will stand by and await orders.

(4) Each section will detail one man to remain behind and collect all material left behind at the battery position and remove it to the Battery S.A. Dump. When this has been done they will remain on guard over this material until further orders.

B (1) When information has been received that the final objectives of the 185th & 187th Brigade have been gained the 186th Brigade will move to the attack & orders to advance will then be communicated to those concerned, when the following moves will take place :—

(a) C Section & a subsection of B section under 2/Lt. J. McFARLANE will move as quickly as possible to about K.7.b.4.6.

Objective 2 guns will support advance of a battalion of 186th Inf Bde from line K15c15.85. to K16.b.4.0. to line K3d6.1. to K4d.5.5. by sweeping HINDENBURG SUPPORT LINE. In the meanwhile the 4 remaining guns will open steady fire on GRAINCOURT.

When the above objective has been gained another battalion will attack GRAINCOURT & all 6 guns will cover this advance by opening intense fire on GRAINCOURT and its approaches.

(b) A subsection of A section under 2/Lt. A.W. SPENCER will advance with the battalion detailed to take the trench N of the BAPAUME-CAMBRAI ROAD & the bridge across the canal

(c) A subsection of A section under SGT CAMPBELL will advance with the battalion detailed to take the Factory in E. 29a on the BAPAUME CAMBRAI ROAD.

(d) A subsection of D section under Lt. R.F.C. OXLEY-BOYLE will advance with the battalion detailed to take GRAINCOURT.

(e) A subsection of B section under 2/Lt. E.W. DENT & a subsection of D section under 2/Lt. D. MILLIKIN will rally at Q36.b.2.2. (BUTLERS CROSS) & form Brigade Reserve.

(3)

(2) As much ammunition as possible must be taken forward in the first instance.

(3) Range finders will be distributed as follows:—
   1 with (1)(a)
   1 " (1)(d)
   2 " (1)(c)

(4) <u>Transport</u> As soon after zero as possible pack animals will be sent forward to enable the guns to advance

They will report as follows:—
   16 mules (8 with pack saddles & 8 with service saddles) and 8 drivers to Q.2.d.2.0.
   16 mules (8 with pack saddles & 8 with service saddles) and 8 drivers to Q.3.b.2.2. (BUTLERS CROSS)

Immediately the advancing guns have reached their destination the mules will be sent back and will return to the above rendezvous.

All animals will carry feeds.

ACKNOWLEDGE.

Issued by hand at 8.30 A.M.

L.B. Mark Capt
C/mdg 213th M.G.Coy

1. ~~File~~
2/3 War Diary
4. ~~Commanding Officer~~
5. Second in Command
6. Lieut R.H. Oxley Boyle
7. 2/Lt D. Mullikin
8. "   E.W. Dent
9. "   J. McFarlane
10. "   C.J. Easton
11. "   A.K. Stirling
12. "   A.W. Spencer
13. "   A.J. Gilston
14. Sgt Campbell H.
15. ~~186th Inf. Bde~~

SECRET.　　　213th Machine Gun Coy　　　Copy No 2
                                                                    6/10/17

Amendment to Preliminary Scheme

Reference B (1)(a)

The 2 guns will support advance of the 2/6th D of W.

The 6 guns will support the attack of the 2/4th D of W. on CRAINCOURT

Reference B (1)(b)

Battalion referred to　　2/5th D of W.

Objectives — all trenches & posts east of Canal in K.3 a & b (exclusive of small portion of HUGHES SUPPORT) K.4.a. E.27.a. b. c & d (exclusive of Canal trench) E.28.a. & C.

Reference B (1)(c)

Battalion referred to　　2/7th D of W.

Objectives — all trenches & posts in K.4.d. & b. (including M.G. emplacement at K.4.a.9.8) E.28.b & d. & E.22 c & d

Reference B (1)(d)

Battalion referred to　　2/4 D of W.

Objectives — To capture CRAINCOURT and FACTORY. & establish posts in a line from E.30.d.3.0. on GRAINCOURT—ANNEUX ROAD inclusive — CEMETERY in E.30.C — E.23.d.y.1. on BAPAUME—CAMBRAI ROAD. & E.23.C.1.6.

ACKNOWLEDGE.

To all recipients of preliminary scheme.

　　　　　　　　　　　　　A.S. Miller
　　　　　　　　　　　　　　　　Lt & Adjt
　　　　　　　　　　　213th M.G. Coy.

SECRET.

18/11/17
L.P. 679

Addenda to Preliminary Scheme.

As soon as possible after the advance of the 186th Brigade has begun an advanced Coy ammunition dump will be formed in the vicinity of the Chapel K.22.d.2.4.

As soon as this dump has been formed all personnel and transport of the Coy moving either forward or returning to the rear will report at this spot.

To all recipients of
Preliminary scheme

R.B. Mark Capt.
Cmdg 213th M.G. Coy.

SECRET.   213th Machine Gun Company   Copy No 2

Preliminary Instructions 2.   15/11/17

1. The C.S.M. will be in charge of the Company Dump at Q.36.b.2.2. (BUTLERS CROSS)

2. All available belt boxes will be taken up to the battery positions but ONLY 12 BOXES PER GUN WILL BE TAKEN FORWARD. The remainder will be collected by the men detailed for that purpose & will be dumped at the Company dump at BUTLERS CROSS & placed in charge of the C.S.M.
   These boxes will form a company reserve.

3. The load for a pack mule doing 25 miles per day is 160 lbs. For shorter journeys loads of 180 lbs are permitted. The weight of a filled belt box complete is about 21 lbs.

4. The load for a pack mule will consist of 6 belt boxes and minor gun material, but neither gun nor tripod will be carried on the animal.
   S.A.A. should be placed in sandbags and carried to make up the full load.
   Wherever possible this should be done by filling spare belts and carrying them in sandbags.

5. Each advancing gun should have not less than 4500 rounds with it. This will be carried as follows:-

   12 belt boxes............ 3.000.
   2 mules each carrying
   10 bandoliers or
   2 belts in sandbags........ 1.000
   6 men each carrying 2 bandoliers 600

                                    4.600

6. 1 pick 1 shovel & 10 sandbags will be taken

(P.T.O

forward with each gun. In addition to this every N.C.O. and man will carry 2 sandbags.

7. Entrenching tool blades will be carried in front
8. Packs will not be carried; haversacks will be carried on the back.
   If leather jerkins are issued these will be carried rolled in waterproof sheets on back of belt under haversack.
9. Every man must take forward his washing and shaving material.
10. Every man will carry one full days ration in addition to his iron ration
11. Foot massage will be carried out daily throughout the operations.

ACKNOWLEDGE.

Issued by hand at 3.15 p.m.
To all recipients of
preliminary scheme & O.S.M.

R.S. Muller, Lieut & adjt
213th M. G. Coy.

SECRET.   COPY Nº 2

Addenda to Preliminary Instruction Nº 2

17/11/17

1. Reference para 8

The issue of leather jerkins not being authorized, greatcoats will be worn. The skirts will be buttoned up. The equipment will be worn over the greatcoat, with the haversack on the back and the entrenching tool in front.

2. The spare part boxes will not be taken but the first aid case will be packed so as to hold one complete fusee spring & one muzzle cup. All tools that may be required will be tied up in a sandbag and attached to the gun case.

3. All oil cases & gun grips will be filled.

4. Sandbags will be drawn from the Quarter-master stores on the scale laid down in para 6 of Preliminary Instructions No 2.

5. Every man will carry the following articles.
        Iron ration
        One days complete ration
        Washing & shaving material
        One clean pair of socks.

6. One full petrol tin will be taken per gun, & one per gun team, the remainder will be handed over to Lieut R. A. T. MILLER.

7. The 30 ft of cord issued today will be used to assist in securing articles on pack animals.

8. All spare belts will be filled & taken up the line in sandbags

9. 3 small aiming posts per gun in addition to the T aiming mark & zero post will be taken.

10. The P. H. helmet will not be carried during forthcoming operations.

ACKNOWLEDGE.   R. H. Miller   Lieut Adjt.
To all recipients of   213th M. G. Coy.
Preliminary Instructions Nº 2

War Diary

213th Machine Gun Company
Daily Orders Part II   No 8 (Page 1)
Nov 29/1917

1. To Hospital

103801	Pte Barham W.	B Section	To hospital	24/11/17
64769	" Cooper A.	A "	" "	26/11/17
102376	" Hemstock E.	A "	" " (Battle Casualty)	27/11/17
81603	" Hume G.	H.Q. "	" "	28/11/17

2. Strength Increase

15286	C.Q.M.S. Steel H.		Joined from 89 Coy 24/11/17
117850	Pte Ashurst W.		Joined from Base 24/11/17
117843	" Good G.		" " " 24/11/17
118071	" Kitson W.		" " " 24/11/17
118842	" Turner T.		" " " 24/11/17
118700	" Turner W.		" " " 24/11/17

3. Postings

117850	Pte Ashurst W.		To A. Section 24/11/17
118071	" Kitson W.		" " " 24/11/17
118700	" Turner W.		" " " 24/11/17
117843	" Good G.		To C. Section 24/11/17
118842	" Turner T.		To D. Section 24/11/17
15286	C.Q.M.S. Steel H.		To H.Q. Section 24/11/17

4. Strength Decrease

64046	Pte McBride D.	A. Section	To U.K. Candidate for commission	24/11/17
3752	C.Q.M.S. Somerset F.	H.Q. "	Promoted C.S.M. and transferred to 15th M.G. Coy	27/11/17
102376	Pte Hemstock E.	A. "	To 48 C.C.S.	23/11/17

5. Casualty in Action Strength Decrease

57991	Pte Page G.	D. Section	Wounded in action	21/11/17

6. Leave to U.K. and Ration Allowance

42395	Pte Brown A.	D. Section	Leave to U.K.	27/11/17 to 11/12/17

(P.T.O

No 8 (Page 2)

7. To Course

	2/Lt	E.W. Dent	B. Section	Veterinary Course	30/11/17
88278	Pte	Waters S.	B	" "	30/11/17
63861	L/C	Greaves G. W.	Trspt	" "	30/11/17

8. Casualties in Action Strength Decrease.

	2/Lt	D. Millikin	A. Section	Wounded in action	27/11/17
102376	Pte	Hemstock E	A	Battle Casualty	23/11/17
68017	L/C	Holskamp W	A	Killed in action	26/11/17
20149	Pte	Duncan G	B	" " "	26/11/17
64754	Cpl	Anderson J	C	" " "	27/11/17
87026	L/C	Sawyer H	C	" " "	27/11/17
102376	Pte	Murray G.	A	Wounded in action	28/11/17
86544	"	Saville E	A	" " "	26/11/17
117850	"	Ashurst W	A	" " "	28/11/17
65547	"	Haynes H.	A	Missing	29/11/17
45559	Sgt	Fulford J	B	Wounded in action	27/11/17
88488	"	Lovett E	B	" " "	27/11/17
46102	Cpl	Fisher H	B	" "	27/11/17
64149	Pte	Appleton C	B	" "	27/11/17
87355	"	Steward J.C	B	" "	27/11/17
64814	"	Garland G.	B	" "	27/11/17
25255	L/C	Flaxman C	C	" "	27/11/17
64154	Pte	Coley J.	C	" "	27/11/17
64320	"	Fisher J	C	" "	27/11/17
81938	"	McLean S	C	" "	27/11/17
54803	"	Penney J	C	" "	27/11/17
81608	"	Pratt V C	C	" "	27/11/17
106650	"	Jones G.	C	" "	29/11/17
66749	"	Thomson W	C	" "	27/11/17
54666	"	Thornley A.	C	" "	27/11/17
67764	L/C	Morrison W	D	" "	27/11/17
68459	Pte	Sleeman N	D	" "	27/11/17
84637	"	Thompson J	D	" "	29/11/17
67997	"	Whitehead J.	D	" "	27/11/17

No 8 (Page 3)

8. Casualties in Action strength Decrease Cont:
64474 Pte Cornwall W H.Q. Section   Wounded in action 27/11/17
54893   " Lawson. T   H.Q.   "   "   "   "   27/11/17
82336   " Ganney S D   "   "Battle casualty shell shock?" 27/11/17

9. Wounded in action (Remained at Duty)
42893 Cpl Cunningham J H.Q. Section   Wounded in action 27/11/17
103120 Pte Shelton G B   "   "   "   "   27/11/17
20100 L/C Shepherd T C   "   "   "   "   26/11/17

R. de la Boyle Lt /o. Capt
Cmdg 213 M.G. Coy.

APPENDIX
No 4
213th M. G. Coy.

NOVEMBER 1917

War Diary

Company Routine Orders
by Capt L. A. Pollad
Cmdg 213th M.G. Coy.

Copy No 3

Roo 2/09/7

No 38. Return from Hospital, courses & leave.

All ranks on rejoining the company from hospital courses, or leave, will report in person to Coy H.Q. In addition Section Commanders will report in writing to the orderly room, when any N.C.O. or man of their section has rejoined.

No 39. Solder - Recovery of.

Arrangements are being made to recover the solder in tins. Accordingly all empty bully beef tins and other tins if they have solder in them will be returned to the nearest Area Commandant for treatment, & not put in the incinerator.

No 40. Leave - Entry of in pay book.

A recent inspection at a Base Port of the pay books of a number of soldiers proceeding on leave revealed the fact that in 24 per cent of the books examined, G.R.O^s 1267 and 2684 had not been complied with.

It is pointed out that it is impossible to ensure the accuracy of the return rendered monthly under A.G. D/1978 of 16/9/17 if these records are not kept up as ordered.

No 41. Leakage of information.

It is forbidden, except in the course of duty, to discuss or refer to any movement of troops, or to the situation of any body of troops, or to operations of any kind whatsoever.

Where evidence is forthcoming that any Officer, Warrant Officer, Non-Commissioned Officer or private soldier has disobeyed this order, he will be tried by Court Martial

No 42. **Cutting of wood.**

    Damage has been caused to woods and forests in the Third Army Area by the indiscriminate cutting of wood by units and individuals without reference either to the owners or to higher authority.

    Wood can only be cut after the necessary arrangements have been made with the owners by the Forest Control Officer, Third Army.

    All applications to cut wood for fuel will be referred through Corps and Divisional H.Q's for Corps & Divisional Troops, & through the R.I.S. & T. of the Army for Army Troops.

    Applications to cut wood for Engineer purposes will be referred through C.R.E's and C.E's to the Forest Control Officer, Third Army.

    It is forbidden to cut wood in the Third Army Area until application has been made, & sanction received, as above.

                               [Signature] Capt.
                       Cmdg 213th M.G. Coy

Hardieang.

Company Routine Orders
by Capt L.A. Pollak
Cmdg 213th M.G. Coy

Copy No 3

6/10/17

No 43. Milk – Local purchase of.
   Fresh milk bought from local farms must be boiled before use.

No 44. Censorship.
   Cases are being reported of infringement of Censorship Orders and Regulations in the Field (SS 393). Letters are being received bearing the designation of both the Unit and Brigade.
   The correct postal address for men of this unit is simply 213 M.G. Coy & this must not be placed at the head of a letter.

L.A. Pollak, Capt.
Cmdg 213 M.G. Coy

War Diary

Company Routine Orders   Copy No 2
by Capt. R. A. Tollak
Cmdg 213th M.G. Coy.   14.12.17

No 45 Detailing of Transport.
All transport requirements other than those detailed by this Office will be submitted to the transport officer who will decide which vehicles are to be used.

Under no circumstances will instructions be issued direct to drivers without the matter previously being referred to, and approved by, the transport Officer.

The fighting limbers & H.Q. limber will never be used for manure fatigue.

No 46 Limber Covers.
All limbers on returning to the waggon lines will immediately have the covers put on, & properly tied down. The driver who has brought the limber back will be held responsible that this is done.

No 47 Solder - Recovery of.
D.R.O. No 970 is held in abeyance while in this area. Units will send tins to the Kilns which are nearest them. These are being erected near the Head quarters of Brigade Groups.

No 48 Christmas Greetings.
There is no objection to the following being written on "Field Service Post Cards":—
"A Merry Christmas and a Happy New Year"
Attention is called to Censorship Orders, para 6, by which the sending of Christmas & New Year cards, photographs, etc, to enemy or neutral countries for letters

No 49 Lanterns, Bullseye.
Approval is given for the issue of lanterns bullseye to Brigade M.G. Coys on a scale of 1 per troop or gun.

Demands in complete to this scale should be noted through O.C.s concerned, & issue will be made as supplies become available.

No 50. Waterproofing Web: Ammunition Belts for MG.

The process described in G.R.O. No 1317 has not proved satisfactory, as waterproofed belts tend to become so sticky in hot weather that they cannot be used.

In future belts will not be treated locally with waterproofing mixture and G.R.O. No 1317 is therefore cancelled.

                       D. Shan Capt
              Cmdg 213th M.G. Coy.

No 31. Discipline.

The practice of using short cuts through private property in Villages is to cease forthwith. Gates if opened for the passage of troops or individuals must be closed immediately.

                       D. Shan Capt
              Cmdg 213th M.G. Coy.

War Diary.

213th Machine Gun Company
Daily Orders Part II

No. 7 (Page 1)
Nov. 22/1917

1. Proficiency Pay – Grant of

The following N.C.O's and men are granted Proficiency Pay Class I, at the rate of 6d per diem, from the dates stated:—

3762 Sgt Campbell R.A. Sect	10/4/17	46102 Cpl Fisher H	B. Sect	1/11/17
20292 " Norman A. "	26/4/17	34874 L/C Speed W	"	22/1/18
67636 Cpl Twigg W. "	17/8/17	87355 Pte Stewart J.C.	"	18/3/18
63017 L/C Holskamp W. "	28/3/18	54803 " Penney J C	"	8/4/18
81497 " Hughes A. "	20/10/17	7144 Sgt Handford S D	"	20/11/16
63206 Pte Clark G "	8/12/17	11289 L/Cpl McLean C	"	18/9/17
26445 " Samways D "	20/10/17	7699 Sgt Murray H	Trspt	19/8/17
47647 " Barrett G.C. H.Q. "	30/3/18	35041 Dr. Foyce W	"	13/3/18
37275 " Burkitt H. "	2/3/18	63359 " Grafton J	"	10/2/18
30286 " Capp C "	8/2/18	54162 " Snook J	"	17/3/18
29468 " Church J "	10/2/18	4202 " Summers J	"	26/4/17

Authority for above R.P. 1/B/P.P./011 d/- 29/10/17

The following N.C.O's and men have been granted Proficiency Pay Class II at the rate of 3d per diem, from the dates stated:—

81498 Pte Joy J	B sect	15/2/17	Authority R.P.1/B/P.P/0.11 d/-29/10/17
5458 " Partridge A C	"	1/5/17	" " " " "
21656 L/C Hudson M H.Q.	"	7/9/16	" " " " "

The Proficiency Pay of the following N.C.O's and men is INCREASED to Class I, at the rate of 6d per diem, from the dates stated:—

81498 Pte Joy J	B Sect	1/7/17	21656 L/C Hudson M H.Q. Sect	1/7/17
5458 " Partridge A C	"	1/7/17	42055 Pte Birchenough J Trspt "	1/7/17
81501 " Robinson A D	"	1/7/17	6344 " Davidson J "	1/7/17

Authority for above R.P. 1/B/P.P./011 d/- 29/10/17

(P.T.O.

APPENDIX
No 5

213th M G COY

NOVEMBER 1917

No 7 (page 2)

2. To Hospital.
63129 Dr Pritchett. J   Trspt Section   To hospital   16/11/17

3. Strength Increase.
37022 Dr Lomas J   Joined from Base 16/11/17
26154 " Smith A   "   "   "   "   16/11/17
88715 Pte Small R.J   "   "   "   "   16/11/17
42032 " Wrigley A   "   "   "   "   16/11/17

4. Postings.
42032 Pte Wrigley A   To A. Section   16/11/17
88715 " Small R.J   " C "   16/11/17
37022 Dr Lomas J   " Trspt "   16/11/17
26154 " Smith A   " " "   16/11/17

5. Strength Decrease.
67775 Pte Wanford A.E.   A. Section   To 8 C.C.S.   13/11/17
64153 " Bird. A.   B "   To " " "   12/11/17
58899 " O'Donnell H.   C "   To " " "   12/11/17
3634 L/C Dale. W.   D "   To U.K. sick   4/11/17
67813 Pte Monk. W.   D "   To 8 C.C.S.   12/11/17
90075 Pte Fisher J.   C "   To 49. " "   14/11/17

6. Attached. (2/6 D. of W)
267675 Pte Callaghan P.   C "   (att) To 8 C.C.S.   12/11/17

7. Attached (2/5 D of W)
245171 Pte Mann J.W.   B "   (att) Killed in action 20/11/17

8. Casualties in Action (Strength Decrease)
7588 Pte Goode W   A Section   Killed in action 20/11/17
65388 " Hawkins. A.   A "   Killed in action 20/11/17

9. Casualties in Action.
63206 Pte Clarke. G.   A "   Wounded in action 20/11/17
81498 " Toy. J.   B "   Wounded in action 20/11/17

                                         Miller. Lt & Adjt
                                         213th M.G. Coy.

War Diary.

213th Machine Gun Company
Daily Orders Part II

No 6 (Page 1)
Nov 15/1917

1. To Hospital.

64453	Pte Bird A.	B. Section	To hospital	12/11/17
58899	" O'Donnell H	C "	" "	12/11/17
267675	" Callaghan P	C " (att)	" "	12/11/17
67813	" Monk W.	D "	" "	12/11/17
67775	" Wanford A.E.	A "	" "	13/11/17
90075	" Fisher J.	C "	" "	13/11/17

2. From Course.

63888	Dr Garrod C	Trspt "	From course	12/11/17

3. Strength Increase.

10809	L/C Hird T.	Joined from Base Depot	10/11/17
20179	Pte Duncan G.	" " " "	" "
106566	" Banner A	" " " "	" "
18499	" Bonar S.	" " " "	" "
106569	" Black R.	" " " "	" "
90075	" Fisher J.	" " " "	" "

4. Strength Increase (Rejoined)

67814	Pte Garland G.	Rejoined from C.C.S.	13/11/17

5. Strength Decrease.

36338	Dr Thorne A	Trspt Section	To C.C.S.	29/10/17
548110	Sgt Attwood A.E.	C "	To 8 " "	6/11/17
64082	L/C Collins C.M.	A "	To U.K. Candidate for commission.	12/11/17

6. Postings.

174154	Sgt Stewart D.	To C Section	4/11/17
10809	L/C Hird T.	" A "	10/11/17
18499	Pte Bonar S.	" A "	" "
20179	" Duncan G.	" B "	" "
90075	" Fisher J.	" C "	" "
106566	Dr Banner A	" Trspt "	" "
106569	" Black R.	" " "	" "
67814	Pte Garland G.	" B "	" "

Transfers
11284 Cpl McKean C   C Section   To D Section 13/11/17

8. Appointments
81450 P/C Newby W.   C "   Appointed A/Cpl 28/10/17
                              vice Cpl Leithead to
                              41 Stationery Hospital 28/10/17

87026 Pte Sawyer H   C "   Appointed unpaid L/C 28/10/17
                              vice L/C Newby app'd
                              A/Cpl

27304 Pte Walker W   D "   Appointed unpaid L/C 13/11/17
                              vice L/C Dale to Hospital

9. Correction.
11289 A/Cpl McKean C   D "   Instructions have been
                                received from the Officer
                                i/c M.G.C. Section 3rd
                                Echelon that the promotion
                                of A/Cpl McKean C to the rank
                                of Cpl is not sanctioned as
                                this N.C.O. was app'd A/Cpl
                                vice Cpl Smith who is still
                                on the strength of substantive
                                N.C.O's of this unit.
                                Daily Orders Part II No 3
                                Page 1 para 1 dated 24/10/17
                                with reference to this N.C.O.
                                is therefore cancelled

10. Punishments & Deprivation of Pay.
28385 L/C Jones D.   Trsp't Section   Being in possession
                                         of a dirty mess tin 8/11/17
                                         Reprimanded   8/11/17

64232 Pte Chamberlain Ab. B "   ⎫ Being in possession
87355 " Steward J.C.   B "   ⎬ of a dirty mess tin 8/11/17
305838 " Walsh J.W.   B " (att)   ⎭ Deprived 5 days pay 8/11/17

200919 " Kuttall J   A " (att)   Absent from 8.30 am
                                         parade 8/11/17
                                         Deprived 5 days pay 8/11/17

267675 Pte Callaghan P C " (att)   Absent from 8.30 am
                                         parade 8/11/17
                                         14 days F.P. No 1 8/11/17

                                         Walker S.M.J. Capt
                                         Cmdg 213th M.G. Coy

War Diary

213th Machine Gun Company
Daily Orders Part II

No 5 (page 1)
Nov 7/1917

1. To Hospital
63899	L/C Wiggins J.	Trspt Section	To hospital	2/11/17
65168	Pte Humphreys A.	D	" "	5/11/17
54840	Sgt Attwood A.E.	C	" "	6/11/17

2. From Hospital
63867	Dr Boddy C	Trspt "	From hospital	4/11/17
63848	" Hurst W	" "	" "	4/11/17

3. To Course
11289	Cpl McLean E.	C "	To M.G. course	6/11/17

4. Punishments
58899	Pte O'Donnell H.	C "	When on active service falling out of the line of march without permission 30/10/17 Deprived 10 days pay	1/11/17

5. Strength decrease
67814	Pte Gasland G.	B "	To 41 Stationary hospt	1/11/17
65168	" Humphreys A.	D "	To 8 C.C.S.	6/11/17
63899	L/C Wiggins J.	Trspt "	To 8 " "	4/11/17

6. Strength Increase (rejoined)
17454	Sgt Stewart D.		Rejoined from Base	4/11/17
63881	Dr Childs R.	Trspt Section	" from C.C.S.	5/11/17
103788	Pte Pultney S.	D "	" " " "	5/11/17

[P.T.O

No 5 Roll

7. Strength Increase

13501	Pte Berriman C.	Trps Section	Joined from Base	4/11/17
60846	" Gallagher C.	"	"	4/11/17

8. Attached

307621	Pte Beck E.	2/4 D of W	To A Section		3/11/17
23875	" Bryan W.	"	"		3/11/17
202347	" Greenwood W.	"	"		3/11/17
260919	" Nuttall J.	"	"		3/11/17
20933	" Simpson J.	"	"		3/11/17
245171	" Mann J.W.	2/5 D of W	To B Section		3/11/17
241352	" Haywood H.	"	"		3/11/17
265127	" Whaites J.W.	"	"		3/11/17
307020	" Ramsay J.W.	"	"		3/11/17
305838	" Walsh J.W.	"	"		3/11/17
267675	" Callaghan P.	2/6 D of W	To C Section		3/11/17
267213	" Stott H.	"	"		3/11/17
268909	" Denton H.	"	"		3/11/17
268352	" Organ W.	"	"		3/11/17
25275	" Batty J.W.	"	"		3/11/17
306821	" Brown J.W.	2/7 D of W	To D Section		3/11/17
306906	" Walton G.	"	"		6/11/17
306924	" Moody G.	"	"		6/11/17
306224	" Banks R.	"	"		6/11/17
26915	" Hallmark C.	"	"		6/11/17

Capt
Cmdg 213th M.G. Coy.

SECRET.

ORIGINAL

Vol 10.

War Diary
of
213th Machine Gun Coy

(Volume 10)

From 1/12/17 To 31/12/17

[signature]
John Capt
Cmdg 213 M.G. Coy

Original

Army Form C. 2118.

WAR DIARY
INTELLIGENCE SUMMARY.
(Erase heading not required.)

213 M.G. Coy.

Place	Date	Hour	Summary of Events and Information	Remarks and references to Appendices
Lock No 7/10/11 Canal du Nord	1/12/17		Coy advanced Coy H.Q. + the Coy together with the transport, situated the transport the day together. HQ were situated Henniere at 9 pm. M. Brigade moved on that day, but with supports, the 68 Brigade in the vicinity of the high ground south of the front line. Capt Pilcher, Lieut Steel & Lieut Stone, with the rest of the Coy outside gun positions at 8 pm. Lieut Bayley, Lieut Steel & Lieut Stone with those guns & Bde machine gunners about there were 3 Lewis guns were in front of... [illegible] ... 10/. Lieut... Coy H.Q. at Quentin	
do	2/12/17		Position we keyed all day. At 4:30 pm Brigade issued order to withdraw via Brig. Pvenier to Leadacourt station. Each mule was rendidly... [illegible] ... as to gun families. Lieut [?] wounded	
do	3/12/17		Still had. Movements were uneventful. [illegible] ... wounded. The withdrawal was completed without further interruption and B. H.S. ... The last of the Coy had left the [illegible] ... at 1.30 am 4/12/17	

Original

Army Form C. 2118.

WAR DIARY
INTELLIGENCE SUMMARY

213 Mech Coy

Instructions regarding War Diaries and Intelligence Summaries are contained in F. S. Regs., Part II. and the Staff Manual respectively. Title pages will be prepared in manuscript.

(Erase heading not required.)

Place	Date	Hour	Summary of Events and Information	Remarks and references to Appendices
LABUISSIERE	4.12.17		Coy entrained at PREMICOURT, detrained at BEAUMETZ-LES-LOGIES and marched to HELLICOURT where it noted into billets at 5pm. Transport came by road and arrived about the same time.	R/
BELLICOURT	5.12.17		Coy moved by road to HABARCQ. CO proceeded on leave to UK	R/
HABARCQ	6.12.17		Coy moved by road to TINCQUETTE arriving at 12.30 pm	R/
TINCQUETTE	7.12.17		Inspection by Section Officers with a view to refitment	R/
TINCQUETTE	8.12.17		Day spent in checking appearance and training Lt R HARRIS upon duty	R/
TINCQUETTE	9.12.17		Day spent in refitment and training	R/
TINCQUETTE	10.12.17		Coy moved by road to VENDIN-LES-BETHUNE	R/ - APP'x 1
VENDIN	11.12.17		Coy employed in training	R/
VENDIN	12.12.17		Training according to programme	R/
VENDIN	13.12.17		Training	R/
VENDIN	14.12.17		Coy moved to LE-HAMEL LENGLET arriving at 11.30 am. Reinforcement of 25 O.R. received	R/ APP'x II

Signed
OC 213 Mech Coy

Original.

Army Form C. 2118.

WAR DIARY
-or-
INTELLIGENCE SUMMARY.
(Erase heading not required.)

2/3 M.G. Coy

Instructions regarding War Diaries and Intelligence Summaries are contained in F. S. Regs., Part II. and the Staff Manual respectively. Title pages will be prepared in manuscript.

Place	Date	Hour	Summary of Events and Information	Remarks and references to Appendices
LEHAMEL	15.4.17		Training according to programme	R/1
LEHAMEL	16.4.17		Church Parade. Reinforcement of 2 O.R. received	R/1
LEHAMEL	17.4.17		Training according to programme	R/1
LEHAMEL	18.4.17		Coy marched from to VENDIN LES BETHUNE	R/1
VENDIN	19.4.17		Coy moved back to TINCQUETTE reoccupied old huts	R/1
TINCQUETTE	20.4.17		Training	R/1
TINCQUETTE	21.4.17		Training. CO returned from leave. Reinforcement 4 O.R. received	R/1
TINCQUETTE	22.4.17		Training. 1 O.R. received as reinforcement	R/1
TINCQUETTE	23.4.17		Church Parade. Bathe	R/1
TINCQUETTE	24.4.17		Training. by Coment	R/1
TINCQUETTE	25.4.17		Christian as Major. 2/Lt GULSTON proceeded on leave. Company had dinners by sections in houses. Supper in the same places	R/1

W. Blom Capt.
O.C. 2/3 M.G. Cy

Original

Army Form C. 2118.

WAR DIARY
INTELLIGENCE SUMMARY.
(Erase heading not required.)

213 M.G. Coy

Instructions regarding War Diaries and Intelligence Summaries are contained in F.S. Regs., Part II. and the Staff Manual respectively. Title pages will be prepared in manuscript.

Place	Date	Hour	Summary of Events and Information	Remarks and references to Appendices
TINCQUETTE	26.11.17		Heavy snowfall prevents much outdoor training. Information received of awards of military medals to L/Cpl Davis, Pte Osborn, Pte Bailey & Cpl Rugby for operations around CAMBRAI commencing on Nov 20th	Appx I
TINCQUETTE	27.11.17		Weather cold but fine. Route march.	Appx I
TINCQUETTE	28.11.17		Training carried out according to programme.	Appx I
TINCQUETTE	29.11.17		D Section supplied with 96 deg. degrees in tactical scheme. A & C Sections on range to test training under action officer.	Appx II
TINCQUETTE	30.11.17		Church Parade.	Appx II
TINCQUETTE	31.11.17		C.O. & Lt BOYLE reconnoitre new front. 2/Lt MACFARLANE awarded M.C. for operations near CAMBRAI. 2 Sections on range. 1 Section tactical scheme. Lt BOYLE Coy. Orders — the afternoon.	Appx III Appx IV copy routine and orderly orders Part 2

A.H.M. Coy
O.C. 213 M.G. Coy

APPENDIX I

December 1917

SECRET   213th Machine Gun Company   Copy No 3
            Operation Order No 15

9/12/1917

1.   The 213th M.G. Coy will move from the XIII Corps Area to the I Corps area tomorrow the 10/12/17

2.   Dress. Marching order without packs haversack will be worn on the back. Steel helmets to be worn. The greatest attention will be paid to smartness of appearance & fitting of equipment. No mufflers to be worn. Sections will march in front of transport. Attention is directed to Coy Routine Order No 30 dated 25/10/17

3.   One blanket per man will be carried on the limbers the remainder will be rolled in bundles of 10 & dumped at the Q.M. Stores by 6 A.M. Transport blankets will be carried on No 3 limber. Limbers will be packed by 6 A.M. Mens packs will be labelled and dumped at Q.M. Stores not later than 6.15 A.M.

4.   Haversack rations will be taken and consumed at 12 noon.

5.   Details regarding Lorries will be issued later

6.   Officers valises will be carried on the limbers and will be packed on them by 6 A.M.

7.   Company will parade ready to march off at 6.45 A.M.

8.   Section Cmdrs will inspect their sections prior to Coy parade

9.   ACKNOWLEDGE

Issued by hand at 6.15 pm

R H Miller
Lieut
Cmdg 213 M.G. Coy

1. File
2/3. War Diary
4. Lieut Oxley Dove
5. " R. Harris
6. 2/Lt T. McFarlane
7. " O.S. Sexton
8. 2/Lt A. Easty
9. " A.K. Styling
10. " A.W. Spencer
11. C. Sm
12. C.2 M.S.
13.

APPENDIX II

213 M.G. Coy.

December 1917

SECRET   213th Machine Gun Company   COPY No 3
                         Operation Order No 16
                                                           13.12.17

1.   Company will leave billets in present area and
will march to CONNEHEM area tomorrow Dec 14th.

2.   Dress Full Marching Order with steel helmets.
The greatest attention will be paid to smartness of
appearance and fitting of equipment. Sections will
march in front of transport. Attention is directed to
Coy Routine Order No 30 dated 15/10/17

3.   Section blankets will be packed on fighting limbers
as on previous occasions. Tpt blankets will not be
carried on the first journey. The front half of H.Q.
limber is allotted to the cooks. Orderly room boxes
will be carried on B3 limber. Officers valises will
be carried on the fighting limbers & will be packed
on by 7.30 am.

4.   Section Officers will superintend packing of their limbers

5.   Coy will parade ready to march off at 9.10 am.

6.   Section Cmdrs will inspect their sections prior to
Company parade

7.   A certain amount of transport will return and
will bring on Q.M. stores and any other kit that
is being left behind

8.   ACKNOWLEDGE.

Issued by hand at 4.30 p.m.

1.   File
2/3. War Diary
4.   Lt Celey Boyle
5.   " R Harris
6.   2/Lt J. McFarlane
7.   " A. Gulston
8.   " C.J. Easton
9.   " A.K. Staley
10.   " R.W. Spencer
11.   CSM
12.   CQMS
13.

                                    R Harris   Lieut
                                    Cmdg 213th M.G. Coy.

APPENDIX III

213 Anti G. Coy

December 1917

Winipeny

213th Machine Gun Company
Daily Orders Part II

No 9 (Page 1)
Decr 7/1917

1. To Hospital

67767	Pte Austin R	A Section	To hospital	1/12/17
97707	" Low A. H.	B "	" "	1/12/17
103488	" Pultney S	D "	" "	1/12/17
59382	" Graves J	D "	" "	1/12/17

2. From Hospital

103801	Pte Barham W	B "	From hospital	6/12/17

3. From Hospital Strength Increase

64230	Pte Fisher J	C Section	Rejoined company	1/12/17
54666	" Thornley A	C "	" "	1/12/17
25255	P/C Flaxman C	C "	" "	1/12/17
117850	Pte Ashurst W	A "	" "	1/12/17
63206	" Clarke G	A "	" "	3/12/17

4. Reinforcements Strength Increase

115233	Pte Gill W	Joined from Base	3/12/17
118083	" McRobb H	" "	3/12/17
118093	" Sankerwitz A	" "	3/12/17
118621	" Waxman H	" "	3/12/17
82042	" Wells J	" "	3/12/17
9135	" Yates W	" "	3/12/17

5. Casualties in Action. Strength Decrease

68002	Pte Cryan J	D Section	Wounded in action	3/12/17
63731	Dr Sutherland D	Trspt	" " "	3/12/17
63881	" Childs R	Trspt	Missing	3/12/17
54389	Pte Fox C. W.	B "	"	3/12/17
88621	" Smith J	B "	Wounded in action	27/11/17

6. Leave to U.K. with Ration Allowance

	Capt L. A. Pollak	H.Q. Section	Leave to UK 6/12/17 to 19/12/17
57478	Pte Jordan J	H.Q. "	" " " 6/12/17 to 19/12/17

Nog (Page 2)

7. To Course
87698 Cpl Plunkett S. A. Section   To M.G. Course 7/12/17

8. Died of Wounds
81938 Pte McLean S. C   "   Died of wounds 29/11/17

9. Postings.
115233 Pte Gill. W.   To B. Section 7/12/17
118093 " Sankerwitz A   "   "   "   7/12/17
118621 " Waxman H   "   "   "   7/12/17
82042   " Wright H   "   "   "   7/12/17
118083 " McRobb H   To C Section 7/12/17
118250 " Wells J   "   "   "   7/12/17
9135   " Yates. W   To D   "   7/12/17
7729 Sgt. Tobson. G.   C Section   To B   "   7/12/17
67636 Cpl Twigg   A   "   To B   "   7/12/17

10. Postings (Officer)
    2/Lt C.J. Easton C   "   To command
                                     B. Section 7/12/17
    2/Lt A.W. Spencer A   "   To command
                                     A Section 7/12/17
    2/Lt E.W. Dent   B   "   To C Section
                                     as sub section
                                     Officer   7/12/17

11. Correction.
65547 Pte Haynes H. A. Section   Previously reported
                                    missing.
                                    To 48 C.C.S. 25/11/17

                                    C.H. Mullis Lieut
                                    Cmdg 213 M.G. Coy.

War Diary

213th Machine Gun Company
Daily Orders Part II

No 10 (Page 1)
Decr 13/1917

1. Strength Increase.

Lieut R. Harris.   Joined from Base 8/12/17
                                                    Authority A.G.
                                                    No AM 66 dt 9/12/17

2. Postings.

Lieut R. Harris   To command
                                                    A. Section   13/12/17

3. Strength Decrease.

103788 Pte Pultney S.   D. Section   To 29 C.C.S   3/12/17
67767 Pte Austin. R.   A   "   To 56 C.C.S   3/12/17

4. From Course.

11289 Cpl McLean C   D   "   From M.G Course 8/12/17

5. Appointments.

63879 Pte Holloway A   Trspt "   Apptd unpaid
                                                    Lance Cpl   13/12/17

6. To hospital.

118041 Pte Kitson W.   A. Section   To hospital   7/12/17
31706 Pte Treadwell E.   D   "   "   "   12/12/17
13501 Pte Berryman C   Trspt "   "   "   13/12/17

R.T. Miller. Lieut
Cmdg 213 M.G. Coy.

"War Diary"

213th Machine Gun Company
Daily Orders Part II — No 11 (Page 1)
20/12/17

1. **Reinforcements. Strength Increase.**

121767	Pte Body S.	Joined from Base 14/12/17
120267	" Braithwaite S.	" " " "
117196	" Cawthan C	" " " "
119280	" Cooke W	" " " "
85585	" Carr B.	" " " "
71976	" Connolly T	" " " "
120291	" Creasdale A	" " " "
119947	" Dillon V	" " " "
120266	" Edge H.	" " " "
119955	" Eames G.	" " " "
119284	" Horsley F.	" " " "
121732	" Hemmingsley J.	" " " "
121752	" Hall A.	" " " "
120216	" Jagger R	" " " "
120296	" Hendrick S.	" " " "
65673	" Loveday E.	" " " "
120299	" Mounsfield A	" " " "
119946	" Ormesher W.	" " " "
121729	" Palmer S.R.	" " " "
121640	" Popple A.	" " " "
117026	" Palmer J.S.	" " " "
121713	" Payne A.	" " " "
42782	Sig Summers A	" " " 16/12/17
103732	Sig Mullender C	" " " "

2. **Postings**

121767	Pte Body S.	To "A" Section 14/12/17
120267	" Braithwaite S.	" " "
120291	" Creasdale A.	" " "
119947	" Dillon V.	" " "
119955	" Eames G.	" " "
120266	" Edge H.	" " "
121752	" Hall A.	" " "

2. Postings Cont:

120296	Pte Hendrick P		To "B" Section 14/12/17
120216	" Tagger R		" " " 14/12/17
65673	" Loveday E		" " "
120299	" Mounsfield A		To "C" Section
119946	" Ormesher W		" " "
121640	" Popple A		" " "
121713	" Payne A		" " "
117026	" Palmer F.C.		" " "
119476	" Connolly J		" " "
85585	" Carr B.		" " "
119284	" Horsley J		To "D" Section "
121732	" Hemingsley J		" " " "
121729	" Palmer S.R.		" " " "
119280	" Cooke W		" " " "
117196	" Cowhan C		" " " "
42782	Sig Summers A		To H.Q. Section 16/12/17
103432	" Mullender C		" " " " "
65542	Pte Merrill J	C. Section	To "B" Section 20/12/17

3. To Hospital

| 67769 | Pte Cooper A | A. Section | To hospital 17/12/17 |

4. From Hospital

| 81603 | Pte Hume G | H.Q. Section | From hospital 16/12/17 |

5. To Courses

| 63888 | Dr Garrod C | Trspt Section | To Vet: course 14/12/17 |

6. From Leave.

| 42395 | Pte Brown A | D. Section | From leave 13/12/17 |

7. Correction.

| 63881 | Dr Childs R. | Trspt Section | Previously reported missing Admitted 6th London Field Amb Shell wound leg 4/12/17 |

A.H. Willis. Lieut
Cmdg 213 M.G. Coy.

Hardiny

213th Machine Gun Company
Daily Orders Part II   No 12 (Page 1)
27/12/1917

1. Strength Decrease

63169	Dr Pritchett F	Trspt Section	To 48 C.C.S.	16/12/17
31706	Pte Treadwell E	D "	To 1 CCS	18/12/17
13501	Dr Berriman C	Trspt "	To 1 " "	14/12/17
67769	Pte Cooper A	A "	To 1 " "	18/12/17

2. Strength Increase (Rejoined)

67775	Pte Wanford A.E	A "	From 8 C.C.S.	20/12/17
63169	Dr Pritchett F	Trspt "	From 48 CCS	22/12/17

3. Reinforcements

122183	Pte Bowman R.		Joined from Base 21/12/17
122460	" Meatyard J.R.		" " " "
122740	" Prosser H.A.		" " " "
122942	" Tooth. W.		" " " "
122438	" Bell. E.		23/12/17

4. Postings

67775	Pte Wanford A.E	To "A" Section	20/12/17
122460	" Meatyard. J.R.	" "B" "	21/12/17
122183	" Bowman R	" "C" "	21/12/17
122740	" Prosser H.A.	" "C" "	21/12/17
122942	" Tooth. W.	" "D" "	21/12/17
122438	" Bell E.	" "D" "	23/12/17
63169	Dr Pritchett. F.	" Trspt "	22/12/17

5. Transfers

42893	Cpl Cunningham J.	H.Q. Section	To C. Section	27/12/17
67763	P/C McDonald. A.	D "	To A "	27/12/17
103765	Pte Hancock A.	C "	" A "	27/12/17
90701	" Dixon J	B "	" Trspt "	27/12/17
44365	" Griffith. J.	B "	" H.Q. "	27/12/17
88276	" Waters S.J.	B "	" C "	27/12/17

6. Leave to U.K. & ration allowance

3762	Sgt Campbell H	A. Section	23/12/17 to 6/1/1918
2/4	A.L. Gulston	Trspt "	25/12/17 to 8/1/1918
64156	Pte Eaton J	A "	25/12/17 to 8/1/1918
27970	Pte Stevenson J.	D "	25/12/17 to 8/1/1918

No 12 (Loe 2)

7. **From Leave.**

Capt L.A. Pollak   H.Q. Section   From leave   21/02/17
57478 Pte Jordan T.   "   "   "   "   20/02/17

8. **From Course.**

63861 L/C Greaves G.   Trspt   "   From Vet course   26/02/17
88278 Pte Waters S. B.   "   "   "   "   26/02/17

9. **Died of Wounds.**

67764 L/C Morrison W. I   Section   Died of wounds   30/02/17

10. **To Hospital.**

15685 Pte Jackson G.A.B.   "   To hospital   22/02/17
2/Lt E.W. Dent   C   "   To hospital whilst on Vet course   22/02/17

11. Proficiency Pay. The Proficiency pay of the following man is increased to Class I at the rate of 6 per diem from the date stated Authority R.P 1/B/PP/1188 d/- 29/10/17

42395 Pte Brown A   D Section   P.P. Class I from   1/7/17

12. **Promotions and Appointments.**

10289 A/Cpl McLean C.   D Section   Promoted Cpl vice 60123 Cpl Leithead (to U.K.) Authority M.G. 3/369 T d/- 5/02/17   22/11/17

81450 A/Cpl Newby W.   C   Promoted Cpl vice 67757 Cpl Anderson (Killed)   26/11/17

67763 L/C McDonald A.D   "   Promoted Cpl vice 46102 Cpl Fisher (wounded) Authority M.G. 1/3935/203A d/- 21/02/17   4/12/17

63891 P/L/C Laws T.B.   Trspt   Apptd A/Cpl vice A/Cpl Newby promoted Cpl   26/11/17

274448 L/C Prested A.   D   "   To receive pay of apptmt vice L/C (A/Cpl) Newby promoted   28/10/17

57504 Pte Pitty T.   H.Q.   "   Apptd Paid L/C vice 68007 L/C Holskamp (Killed)   26/11/17

78499 Pte Bonar T.   A   "   Apptd U/P/Cpl   27/12/17
64156 "   Eaton T.   A   "   "   "   27/12/17
64406 "   Down W.   C   "   "   "   27/12/17
27970 "   Stevenson J.D   "   "   "   27/12/17

No 12 (Page 3)

13. <u>Field Punishment & Deprivation of Pay.</u>

117843 Pte Good G.	C. Section	Stating a falsehood to a N.C.O. 23/12/17 7 days F.P. No 2	24/12/17
26745 Pte Samways D.	A "	Neglect of duty whilst on sentry 23/12/17 10 days F.P. No 2	24/12/17
118250 Pte Wells J.	C "	(1) Absent from tattoo roll call until 8.45pm (2) Not complying with an order given by a N.C.O. 23/12/17 7 days F.P. No 2	24/12/17

J. Khuk Capt.
Cmdg 213. M.G. Coy

APPENDIX IV

2/3 M G Bty.

December 1917

Company Routine Orders
by Capt L.A. Pollak,
Cmdg. 213th M.G. Coy

Copy No 3

29/12/17.

No. 46. Road Control.

Roads are being destroyed by horses going to & from water. Horse watering parties are to proceed to water across country & not along traffic roads. Where necessary O.C. Units concerned must arrange to have tracks made, wire cleared & trenches filled in. When it is necessary to cross a road this should be done as many horses as possible at a time & not in file. When the use of a road by horse watering parties is unavoidable, a report explaining the necessity will be forwarded through the proper channel to Corps.H.Q at once. Whenever possible, horse lines should be placed on the same side of the road as the water troughs allotted to them.

No 47. Method of Registration by Officers in Hotel Visitors' Books in France & Belgium.

An Officer when entering his name in the Visitors' Book in an hotel in France or Belgium will not specify the battalion or other unit to which he belongs. He will, if an Infantry Officer, state his regiment, & in other cases state the branch of the service to which he belongs. No indication is to be given as to the Officer's location in this country other than an entry that he belongs to the B.E.F.

No 48. Leakage of information.

It is forbidden except in the course of duty, to discuss or refer to any movement of troops, or to the situation of any body of troops or to operations of any kind whatsoever. Where evidence is forthcoming that any Officer, Warrant Officer, Non-commissioned Officer or private soldier has disobeyed this Order he will be tried by Court Martial.

No 49. Cutting of Wood.

Damage has been caused to woods & forests in the First Army Area by the indiscriminate cutting of wood by units & individuals without reference either to the owners or to higher authority.

Wood can only be cut after the necessary arrangements have been made with the owners by the Forest Control Officer First Army.

All applications to cut wood for fuel will be referred through Corps & Divisional H.Q. for Corps & Divisional troops & through the R.I.S & T of the army for Army troops.

Applications to cut wood for Engineer purposes will be referred through C.R.Es & C.Es to the "Forest Control Officer" First Army.

It is forbidden to cut wood in the First Army Area, until application has been made, & sanction received, as above.

C H Miller
Capt.
Cmdg 213 M.G. Coy.

War Diary

of

213th Machine Gun Coy.

From January 1st 1916 to January 31st 1918

Volume 11.

O.C. 213th Machine Gun Coy.

Army Form C. 2118.

WAR DIARY
or
INTELLIGENCE SUMMARY

Original 213. M.G. Coy.

(Erase heading not required.)

Place	Date	Hour	Summary of Events and Information	Remarks and references to Appendices
TINQUETTE	1-1-18	12 noon	Coy Training, one Lecture on Tactical talk 2/Lt Br the D/W Regt. Weather cold & fine	K.H.W.
	2-1-18	"	O.C. & Advance party went by motor lorry to decomorile the time returning the same day.	B.H.W.
			Coy Training. 2/Lt M°FARLANE. awarded the MILITARY CROSS. (immediate award) weather cold & fine	B.H.W.
	3-1-18	"	Potential Tactical scheme weather unchanged	B.H.W.
	4-1-18	"	Inspection by Divisional Commander. (I.M.C. & 3MM)	B.H.W.
	5-1-18	"	Coy Training.	B.H.W.
	6-1-18	"	Divine Service. 2/Lt SPENCER. proceeded to Corps Gas School on a 7 days Course.	B.H.W.
	7-1-18	"	Coy Training. Sudden Thaw followed by a very hard frost at night.	B.H.W.
	8-1-18	"	Heavy snow fall. Packing limbers preparatory to move, into new area.	B.H.W.
	9-1-18	"	Coy & Transport entrained at TINQUES FOR MAROEUIL & marched from there to billets in ANZIN. Transport moved by road to ROCLINCOURT. 2/Lt GUSTONE rejoined from leave.	B.H.W. APPEND I
	10-1-18	"	Thaw. Coy Training. Inspection by relief Officer.	B.H.W.
	11-1-18	"	Batta C.O. inspected Coy by Sections. Weather Cold & pier rained.	B.H.W.
	12-1-18	"	Inspection of Batt by Bde A/My Commander in the vicinity of MAROEUIL. 2/Lt SPENCER returned from Gas Course. Weather turning a muggy.	B.H.W.
	13-1-18	"	Divine Service. Cpl PULSUR & HARRIS 2/LT EASTON recommended Coy promotion in the line weather a dew.	B.H.W.
	14-1-18	"	Advance party f/10 men proceed into the line. Coy prepare for going into the line.	B.H.W.

P Owen Capt
O/C 213 M.G. Coy

Army Form C. 2118.

WAR DIARY
or
INTELLIGENCE SUMMARY.
(Erase heading not required.)

Original 213 M.G Coy

Instructions regarding War Diaries and Intelligence Summaries are contained in F. S. Regs., Part II. and the Staff Manual respectively. Title pages will be prepared in manuscript.

Place	Date	Hour	Summary of Events and Information	Remarks and references to Appendices
ANZIN	15-1-18	12 noon	The Coy relieved 208 M.G. Coy in the GAVRELLE Sector & two guns of the 2/2 M.G. Coy in the OPPY section. Very heavy rain throughout the day making the trenches almost impassable. 3 Reinforcements received	APPEND I RM/M
Coy H.Q. in Railway Cutting near BAILLEUL	16-1-18		C.O. went round the line with the D.M.G.O. 2.O.R. in GAVRELLE Post relieved by 2/4 Bn D.o[W].R. Heavy rain. No 8510 RM. THAMES Battery [illegible] 3250 rds in respone to D.o[W].R. S.O.S. call. Rain all day.	RM/M OK/M
	17-1-18		O.C. 2.D.M.G.O. [illegible] the line. 8510 RM. HARRIS to hospital. Cpl. [illegible] & one O.R. wounded at Coy H.Q.	RM/M
	18-1-18		6 O.Rs received. 2 one O.R wounded. THAMES Battery carried out harassing fire during unexposed	OK/M
	19-1-18		6 P.M. & midnight THAMES Battery carried out harassing fire during unexposed	OK/M
	20-1-18		Relief wood relieved. 2nd Lt SPENCER to hospital. Weather mild.	OK/M
	21-1-18		One O.R wounded on working party. Weather milder.	OK/M
	22-1-18		2 O.Rs reinforcements. Weather showery. Coy	OK/M
	23-1-18		2 O.Rs relieved in the line by 208 Coy M.G.C. relief complete by 9 P.M. a working party of 1 N.C.O. & 14 men left at Authay for working party on divisional employment. Sgt JOBSON to U.K. on details.	APPEND II OK/M OK/M
ANZIN	24-1-18		Coy in Billets at ANZIN. Cleaning up & Coy inspection. Div Commander inspected Coy Transport	OK/M
	25-1-18		Coy Commander inspection. Weather bright.	OK/M
	26-1-18		Coy refitting & Baths. Weather bright.	OK/M
	27-1-18		Coy training. Weather colder. Most of the Coy employed on road fatigues.	OK/M RM/M

[Signature] OC 213 M.G.Coy

Army Form C. 2118.

WAR DIARY
INTELLIGENCE SUMMARY

(Erase heading not required.)

Original 213 M.G. Coy

Place	Date	Hour	Summary of Events and Information	Remarks and references to Appendices
ANZIN	28-1-18	12 noon	Coy Training & Troop line instruction. Weather Frosty.	18/4/W
	29-1-18	"	Coy Training & Battn weather unchanged.	12/4/W. C.X.W.
	30-1-18	"	Coy Training & Small Box Respirators tested in Gas chamber. One O.R. proceeded on	C.X.W
	31-1-18	"	a course to MINE SCHOOL at HOUCHIN. Cpl. HARRIS struck off the strength of Coy on being evacuated out of Corps area.	18/4/W

Mohan Cpn
Comdg 213 M.G. Cy

Appendix I
213 rph. y. by

Jany. 1918.

SECRET   213th Machine Gun Company   COPY No 3
Operation Order No 17

8.1.18

Ref Map LENS 11 1/100.000

1. The Company will move into a new area tomorrow Coy & waggon lines will be situated at ANZIN Transport lines   "   "   "   ROCLINCOURT.

2. The Coy will proceed by rail from TINCQUES to MAROEUIL. The transport will move by road march

3. The Coy will parade in full marching order at 9.45 A.M. Greatcoats will be worn, leather jerkins will be worn under greatcoats, steel helmets will be carried in the valise. Special attention will be paid to securing a smart turn out

4. The transport will march off at 8.30 A.M. & move by the ST. POL - ARRAS Road to ANZIN.
Section Cmdrs will detail 2 men to accompany each vehicle (these to include the brakesmen) The transport & the men detailed to accompany the limbers will take haversack rations

5. Blankets & Officers Kits will be packed on limbers by 8 A.M. Section Cmdrs will personally supervise this packing to ensure that it is done tidily & completed punctually.

6. An advance party consisting of L/C HERD, PTE HUTTON & 1 O.R (to be detailed by A. Section) will report at H.Q. 2/7 D of W. Regt. TINCQUES at 8 A.M. & proceed by lorry. PTE HUTTON will take over the transport lines at ROCLINCOURT & then return to the Coy Camp at ANZIN. L/C HERD after taking over the camp will reconnoitre a site for a waggon park

7. One lorry has been allotted to the Coy for transporting Q.M. Stores
PTE BURR. will report at 7.45 A.M. to H.Q. 2/7 D of W

(P.T.O.

TINCQUES & guide the lorry to Q.M. Stores.

Dixies & boilers will be taken on the lorry.

The loading party will consist of:—

   PTE BRACEY
   " BURR
   " NEWELL

These men together with the C.Q.M. Sgt. will travel by this lorry.

8. The Commanding Officer will inspect all billets at 8.30 A.M. Section Cmdrs will ensure that they are left in a scrupulously clean condition.

9. ACKNOWLEDGE.

Issued by hand at 8.30 p.m.

      L. Pollak, Capt
      Cmdg 213 M.G. Coy

COPIES TO:—
1. ~~File~~
2/3 War Diary
4. ~~A Section~~
5. B "
6. C "
7. D "
8. Trspt "
9. H.Q. "
10. C 2 M S
11. ~~11th Inf Bde~~

SECRET

213th Machine Gun Company.
Operation Order No 18.

13.1.18.

Reference map 51ᴮ N.W. 1/20,000

1. The 213th M.G. Coy will relieve the 208th M.G. Coy in the Right Brigade Sector on the 15th inst.

2. The relief will be carried out in accordance with attached table.

3. For purposes of administration the guns in the line will be divided into two groups:—
   (a) TOWY.
   (b) THAMES

To facilitate control O/C B. Section will detail one gun team to be attached to A. Section.

4. At each gun position in the line & each gun in support at Coy HQ. the following stores will be handed over
   - 10 belt boxes
   - 10 boxes S.A.A.
   - 1 tripod
   - 4 Petrol tins { 1 tin for gun, 1 " " team, 2 emergency ration which will be kept at Section HQ }
   - 1 Zero post

Also all other stores such as very light cartridges, Armour piercing bullets, Tracer bullets, and Anti-gas apparatus. Nothing will be taken over by the section in reserve. A list showing stores taken over will be forwarded to Coy HQ. by 6 pm on 15.1.18.

5. All standing & tactical orders, together with maps, defence schemes, night firing tables & aeroplane photographs will be taken over. Every precaution must be taken to ensure that the orders are properly understood by the gun commanders and teams.

The Group Cmdr will personally check the fire orders of his guns & will render a certificate to Coy HQ by 12 noon 16.1.18. stating that this has been done.

Explicit information regarding work in hand or proposed must be obtained.

(P.T.O.

6. The Coy will proceed by light railway from ANZIN (MILL ST LOOP) to CHANTICLER SIDING. Time for entraining to be notified later. From the point of detraining the guns will be man-handled to their positions. No guns will be carried on the shoulder when proceeding through the trenches.

7. One signaller will proceed with each Group Cmdr & will take over telephone at Section H.Q. As soon as relief is complete each Group Cmdr will send back 2 runners to Coy H.Q. one of whom will be retained.

8. Relief will be reported to Coy H.Q. by the word "PIGEON ---- a.m./p.m." the message being sent in the Group Commanders name.

ACKNOWLEDGE

Issued by hand at 10.45 pm

B.H. Mullen Lt. & Adj.
for Capt
Cmdg 213 M.G. Coy.

1. ~~File~~
2/3. War Diary
4. ~~A Section~~
5. ~~B "~~
6. ~~C "~~
7. ~~D "~~
8. Supp "
9. O.C. L.T.M.
10. O.C. T.M.B.
11. ~~208 M.G. Coy~~
12. ~~184 Inf. Bde~~

SECRET.

Table of Relief.

Number of guns	Location	Group	Relieved by	Officer in charge	Rendezvous with guide	Time of meeting guide
1	B.30.c.6.0	TOWY	B Section	2/Lt. EASTON	Junction of TOWY TRACK & RLY CUTTING. B.26.c.1.0	10. A.M.
1	B.30.c.6.1.	"	"	"	"	"
1	B.30.c.55.40	"	"	"	"	"
1	B.30.a.6.6.	THAMES	"	LT. HARRIS	"	"
3	B.30.a.25.40	"	A Section	"	"	"
1	B.24.d.35.40	"	"	"	"	"
4	B.26.b.8.3. (Coy. H.Q.)	SUPPORT	D Section	LT. OXLEY-BOYLE	No guide	"
4	ST. CATHERINES	RESERVE	C Section	2/LT. McFARLANE	"	"

SECRET

213th Machine Gun Company
Amendment to O.O. No 15.

COPY No 2
14/1/18

1. D. Section will relieve two guns of 212th M.G. Coy, location & details of relief will be issued later.

2. C. Section will not relieve section of 208 M.G. Coy at ST. CATHERINES, but will be in support at Coy. H.Q. These alterations may entail further readjustments but these will only be carried out after relief is complete, when detailed instructions will be issued.

ACKNOWLEDGE.
To all recipients of O.O. No 15.
Issued by hand at 12.30. p.m.

R Short Capt.
Cmdg 213 M.G. Coy.

SECRET.   213th Machine Gun Company   COPY No 3
             Operation Order No 19

Reference map 51B NW 1:20000   20.1.18

1.   213th M.G Coy will be relieved by the 208th M.G. Coy in the Right Bde sector on the 23rd inst.

2.   Guides:- One per gun team will report to Coy H.Q. at 3.30.pm. One guide only will be required for the 3 guns in THAMES BATTERY.

     Each guide will be in possession of a slip of paper shewing precisely from which position he comes.

3.   All standing & tactical orders, together with maps, defence schemes, night firing tables & aeroplane photographs will be handed over & receipt obtained. Special care will be taken to ensure that these orders are fully explained to both the section & gun cmdrs. Information regarding work either in hand or proposed will be given in writing.

4.   At each position the following gun material ONLY will be handed over :-
             1 Tripod
             1 Elevating dial
             1 Direction dial
             10 Belt boxes
                Zero post
     All trench stores with petrol cans filled will be handed over.
         At Coy H.Q. the following gun material will be handed over :-
             6 Tripods
             6 Elevating dials
             6 Direction dials
             60 Belt boxes
     Also all stores including 1 Soyers stove

                                                (P.T.O

List of material handed over will be prepared in
duplicate & receipted by the incoming party. One
copy will be forwarded to Coy H.Q. by 9 a.m. 24/1/18
Lieut R.F.C. Oxley Boyle will be responsible for handing
over of stores & material at Coy H.Q.

5. All emplacements, dugouts, shelters, cookhouses
& latrines will be handed over in a tidy & sanitary
condition. Certificates signed by the relieving Coy
stating that this has been done will be obtained &
forwarded to Coy H.Q. by 9 a.m. 24/1/18

6. On relief all gun teams will rally at Coy H.Q.
B.26.b.8.3. whence they will proceed by train to ANZIN

7. Relief will be reported to these H.Q. by the word
"EUREKA   a.m./p.m."

8. Lieut R.A.T. Miller will proceed to ANZIN on the
morning of the 23rd & take over billetting accomodation.
16 Tripods complete with elevating & direction dials
160 Belt boxes & 1 Soyers stove
1/2 limbers will report to Coy H.Q. at 2 pm on
the 23rd.

9. ACKNOWLEDGE

Issued by hand at 9.15 p.m.

[signature] Capt
Cmdg 213 M.G. Coy.

1 File
2/3 War Diary
4 Lt R.A.T. Miller
5 A Section
6 B "
7 C "
8 D "
9 Trps "
10 C.S.M.
11 C.Q.M.S.
12 208 M.G. Coy
13 186 Inf Bde.

Appendix II

213 M.G. Coy

January 1918

War Diary

SECRET   203rd Machine Gun Company   Copy No 3
                Administrative Instructions
                                                10/10/18

Reference map 51b 1/40000

1. **Company H.Q.**
        B.26.b.8.3.

2. **Rations.** Coy rations will be delivered as early as possible each day to Coy H.Q.

    From this point they will be man handled to the gun teams.

    For this purpose all men surplus to 6 per gun team will be despatched at 12 noon daily from their positions to Coy HQ. These men will on arrival at Coy H.Q. be supplied with a hot meal.

    Men & NCOs must be taken in strict rotation so that all benefit by this arrangement. Not more than 50% of the full rank NCO's & 50% of the No 1 are to be sent down on the same day & no gun will be deprived of a full rank NCO & No1 at the same time.

3. **Water.** Water will be drawn from Tanks at
        B.30.a.4.1.
    Water points are available at:
        No 1. B.30.d.6.7.   Right Bn. only
        2. B.30.a.7.7.   Left & Centre Bns.
        3. C.25.a.4.2.

    Movement must be reduced to a minimum at Nos 2 & 3 during daylight.

4. **Ammunition.** Bde S.A.A. Dump Pont-sur-Toir H.qa.9.9.

    Indents for stores will be submitted to Coy H.Q. by 6 p.m. each evening. Stores will not be drawn without indent except in cases of emergency.

5. **Medical Arrangements.**
    Regimental Aid Posts   B.30.a.7.8. B.30.c.6.1.
    Advanced Dressing Station H.4.c.5.4. B.27.a.4.5

6. **Socks.** Section Cmdrs will daily after the change of socks return the soiled pairs by the ration men to Coy HQ. when dry ones will be issued in lieu. Socks for exchange will be sent down in a sandbag together with a note shewing the number returned.

7. **Brigade Canteen.** H d 5 U

8. **Soup Kitchen.** Northumberland Avenue H.4.c.8.3.

9. **Salvage.** As much salvage of every description must be collected as possible. Special attention being paid to petrol tins. All articles salved will be returned at the first opportunity to Coy H.Q.

The importance of salving all material must be impressed on all ranks.

ACKNOWLEDGE

To all recipients of O.O. No 18.

R.W. Wilberforce, for Capt
Cmdg 213 M.G. Coy.

Appendix III
2, 3 N.Z. Bay.

January 1918.

War Diary

To all Officers

No. 213 M.G. Coy.
Date 13/1/18
R.M. 378

13.1.18.

The following points regarding duties when the Company is in the line are republished for information:-

Returns to be rendered.
Daily
(1) Casualty Report. (Battle casualties only; made up to 12 noon. Due at Coy H.Q. 3 p.m.)
(2) Situation Report. (Summary to include all information of interest both positive & negative; direction & nature of wind at time of despatch to be given.)
Due at Coy. H.Q. 10 a.m.
(3) Ammunition Report. (To show (a) No of rounds in belt boxes (b) No of rounds in bulk S.A.A.)
Due at Coy. H.Q. 10 a.m.
(4) Firing Report. (An account of harassing or other fire carried out together with amount of ammunition expended.)
Due at Coy. H.Q. 10 a.m.
(5) Progress Report (A detailed statement of work either improvements or fresh construction carried out with quantities.)
Due at Coy H.Q. 10 a.m.
(6) Food & Feet Report. Due at Coy. H.Q. 10 a.m.
Occasional. Situation report whenever & as soon as anything unusual occurs.

Sentries
(1) One sentry by day, two by night.
(2) All sentries to be properly posted & relieved periodically & visited by a N.C.O. No method of self posting is for one moment to be considered.
(3) All sentries to be conversant with the instructions laid down in memorandum on the subject which is being published separately.
(4) Sentries at all times when on duty to be in a state of alertness. Under no circumstances is eating, reading or sitting down to be permitted whilst on duty.

(2)

When double sentries are on duty one may be allowed to sit down & doze so long as he is within kicking distance of the other, who must be fully alert.

<u>Dress</u> The Box respirator will ALWAYS BE WORN & IN THE ALERT. Skeleton Order, steel helmets will always be worn by all ranks at all times in the front and support line (on this front forward of the red line) Further back men when not on duty may be allowed to remove their equipment.

At "stand to" both morning & evening all ranks will always wear equipment.

Sentries will always wear equipment.

<u>Care of Arms.</u> Guns, rifles & revolvers are to be cleaned twice daily ie. after "stand down" in the morning & before "stand to" at night. Officers will inspect all arms at these times.

Steps must be taken to prevent more than 1 gun in a section be cleaned at the same time.

S.A.A. belt boxes will be carefully examined each day.

<u>Anti-gas Precautions</u>

Box respirators & P.H. helmets will be inspected daily, also anti-gas blankets to ensure that they are in working order.

Each gun position must be in possession of a gas gong.

<u>Sanitation</u> Each gun team is responsible for the state of the trench, both as regards repair & cleanliness for 5 yards on each side of the position.

All dugouts & latrines must be kept in an absolutely sanitary condition.

<u>Discipline</u> Machine gunners will at all times conform to the orders issued to the infantry so far as they are applicable to Machine gunners.

<u>Harassing & Night firing</u> No such firing will take place from the battle position, nor from any spot within 100 yards of the battle position.

(3)

<u>Imparting of Information.</u> Under no circumstances is any information of any military importance especially any referring to the M.G. disposition to be imparted to anyone, no matter what his rank, except by an Officer, & even in this case the officer must take the necessary precautions to ensure that all such information is being passed to the proper quarter. No private or N.C.O. whether on sentry or not, will impart any information whatsoever to anyone, but will refer the enquirer to his section officer.

<u>Shaving</u>
All ranks must be shaved before 9.am each morning

L.P.Much Capt.
Cmdg 213 M.G. Coy

Appendix VIII
213 M.G. Coy

January 1918.

Wagkerry

213th Machine Gun Coy.
Daily Orders Part II   No 3 (eg. 1)
                            3/1/1918

1. To Hospital
7299 Sgt Murray H.   Trnspt Sectn   To hospital   25/12/17

2. From Hospital
7299 Sgt Murray H.   "   "   From hospital   1/1/18

3. Strength Decrease
30286 Sig Capp C.W.   HQ   "   To 56 C.C.S.   3/12/17
59382 Pte Graves J.   Q   "   To 56 C.C.S.   11/12/17
15685 " Jackson G.   B   "   To 42 C.C.S.   24/12/17
97709 " Low A.   B   "   To 56 C.C.S.   18/12/17
67756 Cpl Henderson A. B   "   To 218 M.G. Coy 21/1/18
                                        Authority A.G.C.R.
                                        No. 4612/777 d/ 29/12/17

4. Strength Increase (Rejoined)
67813 Pte Monk W.   From C.C.S.   28/12/17

5. To Course
54111 Pte Thornley A.   C. Section   To Gas Course   30/12/17

6. From Course
63888 Dr Garrod C.   Trnspt "   From Vet Course 30/12/17

7. Postings
67813 Pte Monk W.   To D. Section   28/12/17

8. Transfers
60809 L/C Herd J.   A   "   To H.Q. Section 1/1/18

9. Leave to UK & ration allowance
57022 Dr Lomas J.   Trnspt Sectn   Leave to UK   4/1/18
                                                         to
                                                         18/1/18

                                        L. Black Capt
                                        Cmdg 213 M.G. Coy

2. Field Punishment & Deprivation of Pay   No 03 (Page 2)

64232 Pte Chamberlain A B Sect (1) Found in bed after reveille (2) Stating a falsehood to a NCO. 29/12/17 Deprived 2 days pay 29/12/17

119946 Pte Ormesher W C " Stating a falsehood to a NCO. 29/12/17. 7 days F.P. No 2. 30/12/17

64238 Pte Brown T J D " Absenting himself from his post whilst on sentry 1/1/18 Deprived 7 days pay 2/1/18

119946 Pte Ormesher W C " Conduct prejudicial to good order & military discipline 2/1/18 Deprived 7 days pay 2/1/18

118093 Pte Sankerwitz A B " (1) Hesitating to obey an order (2) Leaving detention without an escort. 2/1/18 10 days F.P. No 1 2/1/18

D. Pink, Capt
Cmdg 213 M.G. Coy.

213th Machine Gun Company
Daily Orders Part II

Notts(?)
10/1/18

1. To Hospital

63717 Dr Davidson J.	Trspt Section	To hospital	7/1/18
120216 Pte Jaggers R.	B	" "	7/1/18
42395 " Brown A.	D	" "	8/1/18

2. From Hospital

118071 Pte Kitson W	A	From hospital	9/1/18

3. To Courses

81479 L/C Hughes. A.	A	To Tump Line course	5/1/18
27304 " Walker W.	D	" " "	5/1/18
2/Lt A. W. Spencer	A	" Gas course	6/1/18
103761 Pte Chiswell	A	Officer's servant	8/1/18
42893 Cpl Cunningham J.	C	To M.G. course	6/1/18

4. From Courses

87698 Cpl Plunkett. S.	A	From M.G. Course	4/1/18
54666 Pte Thornley A	C	" gas course	5/1/18

5. Leave to U.K. and Ration allowance

17454 Sgt Stewart. D.	C Section	Leave to UK	8/1/18 - 22/1/18
67812 Pte Hockett. R.	B	" " "	" "

6. From Leave to U.K.

3762 Sgt Campbell B	A	From leave	7/1/18
2/Lt A. S. Gulston	Trspt	" "	9/1/18
64156 Pte Eaton F.	A	" "	9/1/18

7. On Command

106569 Pte Black R	Trspt	To fetch remounts	8/1/18

8. Proficiency Pay

27970 L/C Stevenson. J.	D	Granted P.P. Class 1 at 6 per diem from 29/9/17 Authority R.P.9/B 1PP/07 dt. 27/10/17	

9. Field Punishments

64232 Pte Chamberlain	B	Being in unauthorized possession of saddle blankets 8/1/18. 14 days F.P. No 1.	8/1/18

(P.T.O.)

No 111 (Page 2)

9. Field Punishments cont:

89594 Pte McCombie J.	B. Section	(1) Being in unauthorized possession of a saddle blanket (2) Concealing a saddle blanket behind a comrade's bed 5/1/18 14 days F.P. No 1 8/1/18

10. Deprivation of Pay

7202 Dr Summers J.	Trops "	Not complying with an order 3/1/18 Deprived 7 days pay 4/1/18
106569 Dr Black R.	" "	Not complying with an order 3/1/18 Deprived 7 days pay 4/1/18

R. Wiley Boyle Lt & Jr Capt.
Cmdg 213th M.G. Coy.

213 Machine Gun Company
Daily Orders Part II   No 15 (page 1)
17/1/1918

1. To Hospital

64475 L/C Chaney. C	B. Section	To hospital	11/1/18
118071 Pte Kitson. W	A "	" "	11/1/18
57275 Sgt Burkett H	HQ "	" "	12/1/18
115233 Pte Gill W.	B "	" "	12/1/18
Lieut R. Harris	A "	" "	15/1/18
103765 Pte Hancock A.	A "	" " Officers Servant	15/1/18

2. From Hospital

120216 Pte Jaggers R.	B "	From hospital	13/1/18
118071 " Kitson W	A "	" "	15/1/18

3. From Courses

2/Lt A W Spencer	A "	From gas course	12/1/18
103761 Pte Chiswell	A "	" " " Officers Servant	12/1/18
81497 L/C Hughes. A.	A "	From Lump line course	13/1/18
27304 L/C Walker W.	D "	" " "	13/1/18

4. Leave to U.K. & Ration allowance.

64401 Pte Condon T.	D. Section	Leave to U.K. 15/1/18 to 29/1/18	

5. From Leave.

27970 Pte Stevenson. T.	D "	From leave (delayed)	13/1/18

6. Strength Decrease

64475 L/C Chaney C	B "	To 30 C.C.S.	9/1/18

7. Reinforcements

39606 Dr Hudson R		Joined from Base	15/1/18
82870 " McDonald W.		" " "	15/1/18
39611 " Malney F.		" " "	15/1/18

8. Postings.

39606 Dr Hudson R.		To Transport Section	15/1/18
82870 " McDonald W		" " "	15/1/18
39611 " Malney F.		" " "	15/1/18

(P.T.O.

9. From Command
105569 Pte Block R.   Deputation   From Boulogne 10/4

10. Proficiency Pay
60846 Dr Gallagher E   Proficiency Pay
    awarded to Classical Proft [?]
    as being R.P. Wagoner [?]

    [signature]   [?]
    O.C. Mt. C. Coy.

War Diary

213th Machine Gun Company
Daily Orders Part II   No 6 (Page 1)
24/1/1918

1. **To Hospital.**

121713	Pte Payne A.	C. Section	To hospital	17/1/18
	2/Lt A. W Spencer	A "	" "	20/1/18
103461	Pte Cheswell J.	A "	" "	20/1/18
106569	Dr Black R.	Trspt "	" "	18/1/18
118842	Pte Turner J.	D "	" "	22/1/18

2. **From Hospital**

63747	Dr Davidson J.	Trspt "	From hospital	08/1/18
37275	Sgt Burkitt H.	H.Q. "	" "	22/1/18

3. **Casualties in Action Strength Decrease**

121729	Pte Palmer J.R.	D Section	Wounded in action	18/1/18
118083	" McRobb M	C "	" "	20/1/18

4. **Strength Decrease.**

	2/Lt E. W. Dent.	C "	To No 2. Stationery Hospital 22/12/17 Struck off strength Authority A.G.M.G. 1/14702 A of 15/1/18	15/1/18
42395	Pte Brown A.	D "	To No 2 C.C.S.	16/1/18
121713	" Payne A.	C "	" "	20/1/18
7729	Sgt Jobson G.	B "	To U.K. Candidate for Commission	25/1/18

5. **To Course**

81899	Pte Aiken. G.	A "	To Sanitation Course	25/1/18
81603	" Hume G.	H.Q. "	" "	25/1/18

6. **From Leave to U.K**

174454	Sgt Stewart D.	C "	From leave	23/1/18
67812	Pte Hockel N.	B "	" "	23/1/18

7. **Leave to U.K. & Ration Allowance**

63891	Cpl Laws J.B.	Trspt section	Leave to U.K.	19/1/18 to 2/2/18
67759	Pte Coaks J.	A "	" "	25/1/18 to 8/2/18

8. **Reinforcements.**

24053	Sgt Calfe W.R.		Joined from Base	18/1/18
7726	" Marjoribanks G.		" " "	18/1/18

No 16 Page 2

8. Reinforcement cont:
124422	Pte Boutcher J	Joined from Base	18/1/18
124593	" Bramley W.	" " "	18/1/18
124483	" Buchanan W.	" " "	18/1/18
124418	" Clinch J.	" " "	18/1/18
29065	Sgt Pymont J	" " "	22/1/18
115248	" Sayce H.	" " "	22/1/18

9. Postings
24053	Sgt Calfe W.R.	To C Section	24/1/18
7726	" Marjoribanks W.	" D "	24/1/18
29065	Sgt Pymont J	" HQ "	22/1/18
115248	" Sayce H	" " "	22/1/18
124422	Pte Boutcher J.	" D "	24/1/18
124593	" Bramley W.	" D "	24/1/18
124483	" Buchanan W.	" B "	24/1/18
124418	" Clinch J	" B "	24/1/18

10. Transfers.
54086	Sgt Darbyshield. D. Section	To B Section	24/1/18
428893	Cpl Cunningham C "	" B "	24/1/18

11. Promotions & Appointments
67636	Cpl Twigg B Section	To be A/Sgt vice 7729 Sgt Jobson to U.K. candidate for commission	25/1/18
63891	A/Cpl Laws F.B. Trspt	To be Corpl vice Cpl Henderson A Trsfd to 206th M.G.Coy Authority A.C.14612/777 C d/. 29/12/17	2/1/18
84874	Pte Speed. W. B	To be A/Cpl vice A/Cpl Laws promoted & further vice 73779 Cpl D. Smith	2/1/18
64406	Pte Down W. C	To be A/Cpl vice Cpl Twigg appted A/Sgt.	25/1/18

11. Promotions & Appointments cont:

Sgt. y.a.R. Hughes A. A/Sectn To receive pay of a Sgt. 24/9/18
                               to complete establishment.

54666 Pte Thornley.a.   C.   " To be unpaid L/C   24/9/18
103042 "   Gray. N.   D.   "   "   "   24/9/18
82042   "   Wright N. B.   "   "   "   2 -10/18

12. To Hospital
121767 Pte Body S   a   "   To hospital   24/9/18

L.Shirk
Capt
O.mdg 213 M.G. Coy

War Diary.

213th Machine Gun Company,
Daily Orders Part II

No 17 (Page 1)
31/1/1918.

1. To Hospital.

37022 Dr Lomas F.	Trpt Section	To hospital, Manchester, whilst on leave to U.K. Auth: Off. i/c M.G. Records R.Cup/12521 C. of 23/1/18		15/1/18
122438 Pte Bell E	D	"	To hospital	26/1/18
121752 " Hall A	A	"	"	26/1/18
26154 Dr Smith A	Trpt	"	"	27/1/18
118093 Pte Sankerwitz A	B	"	"	28/1/18
L/R.F.C. Oxley Boyle. MC.	D	"	"	28/1/18
81478 Pte Simons F (Frain Fermond)	D	"	"	29/1/18
121732 " Hemingsley J	D	"	"	30/1/18

2. From Hospital

103765 Pte Hancock A. (Officers Servant)	A	"	From hospital	27/1/18

3. Strength Decrease.

121767 Pte Body S.	A	"	To 42 C.C.S.	25/1/18
Lieut R. Harris	A	"	" Base hospital	27/1/18

4. Leave to U.K. & Ration Allowance.

67636 Sgt Twigg W	B Section	Leave to U.K.		30/1/18 to 12/2/18
54917 L/Cpl Foster P.	H.Q.	" " " "		30/1/18 to 12/2/18

5. Appointment.

64370 Pte Buchanan E.M.G.	"	Appointed 4/L/Cpl		31/1/18

6. Field Punishment & Deprivation of Pay.

39611 Dr Malney F	Trpt Section	(a) absenting himself from parade (b) making an impertinent reply to a N.C.O. 29/1/18 — 14 days F.P. No.1.	29/1/18

Capt.
Cmdg. 213th M.G. Coy.

Secret

ORIGINAL / WD 12

War Diary

of

213th Machine Gun Company

Volume XII

From 1.2.18   To 28.2.18

Roman Capt
Cmdg 213th M.G. Coy

ORIGINAL
VOL XII
213 Machine Gun Company

WAR DIARY
or
INTELLIGENCE SUMMARY.

Army Form C. 2118.

(Erase heading not required.)

Instructions regarding War Diaries and Intelligence Summaries are contained in F.S. Regs., Part II. and the Staff Manual respectively. Title pages will be prepared in manuscript.

Place	Date 1918	Hour	Summary of Events and Information	Remarks and references to Appendices
ANZIN	3.6.1		Weather Cold - Capt Pollock interviews G.O.C re Coy - Company on range practice on MAROEUIL Range.	
"	2		Weather Bright Frost - Coy railway relieved 205 M.G. Coy in GAVRELLE sector - Relief complete 9.30 pm - Capt Pollock march order No 20	
ARRAS	3		Weather Bright very cold - Coy in the line - Capt Pollock visits Brigade re new H.Q.	
"	4		Weather Mild - Coy in the line - Capt Pollock visits positions with D.M.G.O.	
"	5		Weather Bright - Coy in the line	
"	6		" Mild & sunny	
"	7		" Dull & raining - Coy relieved by 169 Coy - Coy bivouacked at ?	
ANZIN	8		Weather Bright & Cold	
"	9		" Bright & mild - Coy marched to MAROEUIL - entrained the M.M.? train No 2 & detrained on TINQUES - marched to billets at MARQUAY	
MARQUAY	10		Transport by road.	
"	11		Weather Bright - Coy training - N.C.O on gas course	
"			Weather Dull & windy - Coy marched to TINQIETTE - Lt Miller transferred to O.C. 171 M.G. Coy. 2/Lt EASTON sick to UK	
TINQETTE	12		Weather Cold & dull - Coy training	
"	13		Weather Damp & cold - Coy training	
"	14		Weather Raining & cold - Coy training	

J.B. R Brown
Army 213 M.G. Coy

WAR DIARY or INTELLIGENCE SUMMARY

Army Form C. 2118.

Vol XII — 213 Machine Gun Company

Place	Date	Hour	Summary of Events and Information	Remarks and references to Appendices
TINQUETTE	1915			
	15		Weather Dull & cold – 1 NCO to CAMIERS COURSE – 1 NCO to General Headqrs on horsemanship – 2 Lieuts on King's Dispatches & Coy M.G. training	
"	16		Weather Bright, cold. A fat L. day on recent manoeuvres by Brigadier J.M.G. 2 O.R. reinforcements.	
"	17		Weather Cold – Coy Parade to Church Lt N.V. WILLIAMS joins Coy. M.G. on 2nd in command	M.G.
"	18		Weather Cold & bright – Coy training	M.G.
"	19		Weather Cold & bright – Coy our Company gave review parade	M.G.
"	20		Weather Rainy – Coy training	M.G.
"	21		Weather Bright – Coy bathing – Lecture to all Officers of Bn by M.G. Part II G.O.C. Divn – all officers invited	overseas Supplement
"	22		Weather Very windy – Coy training – 20 O.R. on leave to U.K. – Capt POLLAK, Lt BROWNING & Lt STIRLING sit grade for the Corps M.G. Position of M.G. Bureau (BAILLEUL AREA)	M.G. M.G.
"	23		Weather Mild – Coy training	
"	24		Weather Fair – Coy parade for Brigade service – 1 NCO to Procaira – M.G. 1 NCO to A.A Course	
"	25		Weather Cold & sunny – Coy training – Capt POLLAK attends conference of Bn M.G. Coy Commanders by Col. HARRISON D.S.O. M.G. Battn M.G.	
"	26		Weather Sunday – Coy training – Bn HORSE SHOW held at HERLEN–LE–M.G. VERT – 12/13 GOLSTON to Hospital	
"	27		Weather Mist – Coy bathing – 9 officers & 9 men to General Cmdg – 50 R.S. M.G. reinforcements	
"	28		Weather Fine – Coy proceeds to ECOIRE by train – trans of Equipment to M.G. Part II Camp by H.T.S O/C M.G. Coy – transport by road	overseas

Oliver Capt
O/C 213 M.G. Coy

213 M G Coy.

Appendix No 1

Volume 12
February 1918.

SECRET.   213th Machine Gun Company.   COPY No. 2
            Amendments & Addenda to
            Administrative Instructions,
             — dated 14/1/18 —

Reference Map 51B 1/40.000   1/2/18
  Paras. 1, 3, 4, 5, 7, 8 & 9 remain unaltered.
  Paras. 2 & 6 are cancelled & the following instructions
are issued.
2. <u>Rations</u>. Rations for all the teams in the line & Groups
H.Q, will be sent up each night by limber to B 30 a 4.1,
from which point they will be drawn by ration parties
detailed by Group Commanders.
          Rations for H.Q & the 2 teams in reserve
will be sent up as during the previous tour.
6. <u>Socks</u>. Soiled socks will be sent down to Coy H.Q.
each morning by the runner bringing the returns,
when an equal number of dry socks will be sent
up in exchange. The runner must bring a slip
showing the number of socks returned.
10. <u>Runners</u>. The employment of runners will be
reduced to a minimum. All the returns called
for in R.M. 378, d/- 13/1/18 will be sent down by the
morning runner who must reach Coy H.Q. by 9am.
11. <u>Food & feet Report</u>. Special attention must be paid
to ensure that the instructions regarding this matter
are properly carried out & that the rendering of the
returns does not develope into a mere matter of
form. Gun Cmdrs' certificates are attached &
must be kept most strictly & inspected & initialed
daily by the Group Cmdr. As many hot meals as
possible must be provided & every advantage taken of the
Bde. Soup Kitchen
ACKNOWLEDGE   R.F. Willett Mjr, Capt
To all recipients of OO. 20.   Cmdg 213th M.G. Coy

213 M.G. Coy

Appendix No 2

Volume 12

February 1918

be taken over. Every precaution must be taken to ensure that the orders are properly understood by the gun cmdrs. & teams. Explicit information regarding work in hand or proposed must be obtained.

Group Commanders will personally check the fire orders of their guns & will enter them on the Order form which are attached. A certificate stating that this has been done will be rendered to Coy. H.Q. by 6pm 4.2.18.

6. The Coy will parade at 2.45 pm on Company Parade Ground & will proceed by light railway from MILL ST. LOOP to CHANTICLER SIDING where they will detrain & proceed by groups to their positions. All gun material will be taken by train & manhandled from point of detraining to the positions. Rations for the 3rd will also be taken.

7. Two limbers will be detailed to take M.G. material from Coy. H.Q. to the level crossing where they will await the arrival of the Coy. They will report at Coy. H.Q. at 2.30 pm.

8. One signaller will proceed with a D3 telephone with the RIGHT & CENTRE GROUPS COMDRS. & take over from the signallers of 208th M.G. Coy at GROUP H.Q.

O.C. RIGHT & CENTRE GROUPS will each detail two runners for duty at Coy. H.Q. O.C. LEFT GROUP will, on completion of relief, send two runners to Coy. H.Q. one of whom will be returned to Group H.Q.

9. Relief will be reported to Coy. H.Q. by the word "TANDEM" .... A.M./P.M.

10. ACKNOWLEDGE.

Issued by hand at 4.30 pm.

L. Rahar, Capt.
Cmdg. 203rd M.G. Coy

1. File
2/3 War Diary
4. "A" Section
5. "B" "
6. "C" "
7. "D" "
8. Inspn.
9. C.S.M.
10. C.Q.M.S.
11. 208th M.G. Coy
12. 186th Inf. Bde.

SECRET.

Table of Relief.

No. of Guns	Location	Group	Relieved by	Officer to	Accommodation for reserve	Remarks
1	H6a 55.85	Right	"B" Section	7/5 Howitzer Bh gun position		
1	B30c 6.1	do	do	do	do	
1	B30c 5.7	do	do	do	do	
1	B29d 75.30	do	"D" Section	do	Naval trench persons quar.	
1	H5b 90.55	do	do	do	Shipston position	do
1	B30a 55.65	Centre	"A" Section	7/5 Shirley Bh gun position	do	
3	B30a 25.70	do	do	do	do	Thomas Barry
1	B29b 6.4	do	"D" Section	do	Thomas Betty Reserve guns	
1	B29c 75.95	do	do	do	Gummings position	do
1	B25d 25.40	Left	"C" Section	7/5 Mc Farlane Bh gun position	do	
1	B24d 2.7	do	do	do	do	
1	B24d 2.9	do	do	do	do	
1	coy. H.Q.	Reserve	"B" Section	Coy. A.Q.	do	
1	do	do	do	do	do	

213 M.G. Coy

Appendix No 3

Volume 12

February 1918

SECRET.   213ᵗʰ M G Coy   COPY No. 2

Defence Scheme
of
Right Brigade, M. G. Coy.

Reference Secret M.G. Map (Point-du-jour
            Oppy combined sheet) 1/10000

1. "The Brigade Area will be defended at all costs & no portion of the ground will be yielded to the enemy."
The defence of the Area depends in a large measure on the machine guns & they will be fought to the last irrespective of the action of other troops.
All positions have been selected with a view to obtaining effective cooperation & since they are inter-dependent no gun will be moved or its lines of fire altered without the sanction of higher authority.

2. The guns of the Company are distributed as follows

(a) 10 in or about NAVAL & MARINE Trenches (the main line of resistance)

These guns occupy the positions
BIRMINGHAM	BURNLEY
BOSTON	BELTON
BRADFIELD	BUXTON
BARNSTABLE	THAMES BTTY (3 guns)

(2)

To these guns is allotted the task of defending

(1) The outpost line (assistance is given by the guns of the Left Bde. Coy. & the Div. Coy.).

The action of the machine guns in the defence of this line is to put down a barrage between the posts. All these guns have barrage or S.O.S. lines details of which are given on the attached table.

(2) The main line of resistance

For the defence of this line the guns will use direct fire. The directions of the battle lines, by the use of which the most effective results may be anticipated, are also given on the attached table.

(b) In dugouts close to reserve positions

(1) Two of these gun teams complete with equipment are located in a dugout in NAVAL Trench, B.30.c.6.0. In the event of a hostile attack either launched or anticipated, these teams will occupy positions 1 & 4.

(2) 2 teams complete with equipment are located at THAMES Battery, & would, under similar circumstances, occupy positions 6 & 18

(c) 2 guns at Coy. H.Q.

In the event of a hostile attack either

launched or anticipated these teams would occupy positions 7 & 8

Each of the positions mentioned in (b) & (c) is complete with battle emplacement, splinter-proof shelter & 5 boxes S.A.A. The battle lines for the positions mentioned in (b) & (c) are given on the attached table

3. The Corps S.O.S signal is a RED-GREEN-RED chain rocket. There is also a special M.G. S.O.S. consisting of 3 WHITE Very lights fired in quick succession from GAVRELLE post back towards the main line of resistance.

Fire will be opened on S.O.S lines
(a) when either of the above S.O.S signals are displayed
(b) if an S.O.S call is received by 'phone
(c) in the event of the enemy putting down a heavy barrage
(d) if our own artillery opens fire on its S.O.S lines

Rate of fire for S.O.S barrage
    1 belt per min. for 3 minutes
    then 1 " " 3 " " 8 "
    " 1 " " 5 " till situation clears

4. Fire will be opened on battle lines

(a) by the guns mentioned in para. 2(a)

(4)

(1) when it is known that the enemy have penetrated the outpost line
(2) as direct targets present themselves

(b) By the guns mentioned in para. 2(b)
(1) when it is known that the enemy have penetrated the main line of resistance
(2) as direct targets present themselves

(c) By the guns mentioned in para 2(c)
(1) when it is known that the enemy have penetrated the RED line
(2) as direct targets present themselves

Rate of fire for
(1) circumstances mentioned in paras. 4(a)(1) 4(b)(1) & 4(c)(1)
    1 belt per 5 min. till situation clears
(2) circumstances mentioned in paras 4(a)(2) 4(b)(2) & 4(c)(2)
    Rapid until target is annihilated.

5. Company H.Q. are located at H.1.d.4.7.

For purposes of administration & control the guns are divided into Groups, the composition of which is as shown on the attached table.

6. Communication between Coy. H.Q. & Bde H.Q. is by 'phone & runner. Communication between Coy H.Q. & Groups H.Q. is by runner.

"Telephonic communication is established between the Right & Centre Groups' H.Q. & between these H.Q. & Bde. These lines are however, only to be used for sending the S.O.S call, but will nevertheless be tested frequently.

7. In the event of a hostile attack the Coy. Comdr. will immediately report in person to Bde H.Q.
In the above event the Transport Officer will be at once notified & he will report at Coy. H.Q. with the least possible delay with a convoy of 16 pack animals

8. All First Army Trench Standing Orders for Machine Guns will be observed rigidly

L.P. Knox Capt.
Cmdg. 213th M.G. Coy

1. File
2/3 War Diary
4. Right Group Cmdr
5. Centre "
6. Left "
7. Transport Officer
8. 186th Inf Bde
9. D.M.G.O. 62nd Divn
10. Relieving Coy

Administration Table

Group	Guns	H.Q.
Right	Birmingham Boston Bradfield Reserve Gun No 1. " " " 4.	B 30 c 6.0.
Centre	Barnstable Thames Batty (3 guns) Reserve Gun No 6 " " " 18	B 30 a 2.6.
Left.	Burnley Belton Burton	B 24 d 2.7.

SECRET.

213th M.G. Company.

S.O.S. and Battle Lines.

Name	Location	S.O.S. Target	S.O.S. T.B.	S.O.S. C.E.	Battle T.B.	Remarks
Birmingham	H.6.a. 55.56	C.25 a. 65.30	47°	98°	21°	
Boston	B.30 c. 6.1	C.25 a. 95.85	30°	98°	128°	
Bradfield	B.30 c. 5.7	C.25 a. 7.5	70°	72°	125°	
Barnstaple	B.30 a. 53.65	C.25 a. 7.6	91°	34°	125°	
Thames Head	B.30 a. 2.6	C.25 a. 8.8	102°	61°	115°	For height contours to judge
" Centre	do	C.25 a. 75.30	95°	61°	—	25yds contour to judge
" Left	do	C.25 a. 7.5	94°	61°	—	Poor field of fire
Burnley	B.25 d. 25.40	C.25 a. 70.55	120°	Nil	52°	
Belton	B.24 d. 2.7	C. 19 a. 7.1	74°	19°	38°	
Burton	B.24 d. 2.9	C. 19 a. 70.15	51°	10°	128°	
No 1 Reserve	H.5.b. 90.55				120°	
" 4 "	B.29 a. 75.45				25°	
" 6 "	B.29 b. 45.45				125°	
" 18 "	B.29 c. 75.95				32°	
" 7 "	H.4 d. 25.40				25°	
" 8 "	H.4 d. 15.45				63°	

<u>Secret</u>   4.2.13
<u>Amendment to Defence Scheme</u>

The location of BURNLEY as shown on
'S.O.S. and Battle Line' table should
read B24 & 25.40

R Ronan Capt.
Cmdg 213 M.G. Coy.

213 M G Coy

Appendix No 4

Volume 12

February 1918

213th Machine Gun Company
Daily Orders Part II

No 18 (page 1)
7/2/18

1. To Hospital
113071 Pte Kitson W A Section To hospital 5/2/18
103120 " Shelton G J B " " 5/2/18

2. To Course
85585 Pte Carr B C " To mined dugout course 31/1/18

3. From Course
81603 Pte Hume G H C " From course 7/2/18
81899 " Akers G A " " 7/2/18
42893 Cpl Cunningham B " " 7/2/18

4. Reinforcement (Strength Increase)
2/Lt B. Brown Joined from Base 3/2/18

5. Strength Decrease
26154 Dr Smith A Tpt Section To 42 C.C.S 29/1/18
122438 Pte Bell E D " 43 " 31/1/18

6. Leave to U.K. & ration allowance
71544 Sgt Handsford J D Section Leave to U.K 5/2/18 to 19/2/18
64406 Cpl Down W C " " 5/2/18 to 19/2/
82373 Pte Leavicur F B " " 5/2/18 to 19/2/
55887 " Rafters J A " " 5/2/18 to 19/2
58734 " Simison N C " " 5/2/18 to 19/2
81899 " Akers G A " " 5/2/18 to 19/2
7699 Sgt Murray H Tpt " " 7/2/18 to 21/2
64763 Cpl McDonald A " " 7/2/18 to 21/2/
37275 Pte Burkitt H H.Q. " " 7/2/18 to 21/2/

7. From Leave
63891 Cpl Laws F B Tpt " From leave to U.K. 3/2/1
64401 Pte London J D " " 7/2/1

8. Posting
2/Lt B. Brown To A Section 3/2/1
(In command)

No 18 (page 2)

... D Section — Appointed a/Sgt vice Sgt Attwood to hospital, & not vice Sgt Jolson as stated in Daily Orders 6/11/17 1?, No 16 of 24/1/18 (Auth:- A.G./3935/448A) of 1/2/18

" "/L.Cpl D   "   "   L Section — To be a/cpl vice Cpl Twigg appointed a/Sgt (Auth:- A.G. 6/11/17 /3935/448A of 1/2/18)

Honours & Awards
4 Sgt Stewart D. E Section — His Majesty the King has approved of the award of the Belgian Decoration "CROIX-DE-GUERRE" Ref: D.R.O. No ? of 2/2/18

[signature]
213 ...

SECRET.   213th Machine Gun Company   COPY No. 3
            Operation Order No. 20.

Reference Map 51B N.W. Ypres.   1. 2. 18.

1. The 213th M.G. Coy will relieve the 208th M.G. Coy in the Right Bde Sector on the night of the 2nd/3rd inst.
    The present dispositions of 208th M.G. Coy. will be taken over with the exception that only 2 guns will be in Reserve at Coy H.Q. instead of 6. The other 4 guns will move into dugouts in proximity to Reserve position.

2. The relief will be carried out in accordance with attached table.

3. For purposes of administration the guns will be divided into 3 groups:-
    (a) RIGHT.
    (b) CENTRE.
    (c) LEFT.

4. At each position in the line, all trench stores will be taken over, also the following gun material:-
    1 Tripod, complete, with elevation & direction dials.
    10 Belt Boxes
    Aiming Posts
    At Coy H.Q. all stores will be taken over, and the following gun material:-
    6 Tripods, complete, with elevation & direction dials.
    60 Belt Boxes
    A list showing stores and gun material taken over will be forwarded to Coy H.Q. by 9 am, 3.2.18.

5. All standing & tactical orders, together with maps, defence schemes, night firing tables & aeroplane photographs will
                                                        (P.T.O.

SECRET. 213 Machine Gun Company, COPY No 2
Operation Order No 22.

Reference Map Lens 11 1/100.000   8·2·18.

1. The 213th Machine Gun Company will move to MARQUAY on the 9th inst.
    (a) The personnel will proceed by train from MAROEUIL to TINCQUES.
    (b) The transport will proceed by road march.

2. The Company, less transport, will parade at 11 am. Dress:- full marching order, great coats & field service caps will be worn, the steel helmet being carried in the valise. Section Cmdrs. will take effective steps to ensure that all traces of mud are removed from the clothing, that the equipment is clean & all brass work polished. Waterbottles will be filled & haversack rations carried.

3. The blankets of the gun teams & H.Q. section and Officers' valises will be on the limbers by 8 a.m. These will be carried on the fighting & H.Q. limbers only. Blankets will be folded, not rolled. Each section will draw from the C.S.M. 8 horse rugs; these will be folded & packed 4 on each fighting limber on top of the blankets; 2 rugs will be carried on both the H.Q. limber & water cart. Section Cmdrs, will, by personal supervision ensure that when complete, the limbers present a smart appearance & are properly balanced.

All cooking utensils, together with Officers' & Sergts' mess boxes will be packed in the cook's cart by 8.30 am.

The stationery boxes will be carried in the H.Q. limber & will be in position by 8 am.

4. All billets, cookhouses & latrines, will be left

(2)

in a clean & sanitary condition & will be inspected by the C.O. at 9.30 a.m.

5. The following transport has been allotted to the Unit for moving the Q.M. Stores & spare kit & will report at the transport lines at 8.30 a.m.
        1 G.S. Wagon.
        4 L.G.S. Wagons.
   A loading party of 4 men will report in full marching order to 2/Lt CUESTON at the transport lines at 8.15 a.m.

6. 2 men per section will be detailed as brakesmen for the fighting limbers. 1 Signaller will be detailed as brakesman for H.Q. limber. The Church will act as brakesman for the water cart. The brakesmen for the No 3 limbers & the extra wagons will be detailed from the loading party by the Transport Officer. Brakesmen will place their packs on the limbers to which they are attached

7. The transport will move off as soon as the loading is complete. Dress:- Full marching order, great-coats, service caps. The steel helmets will be carried in the saddles. Mid-day feeds will be carried.

8. The signallers will proceed independently by bicycle, reporting on arrival at their destination to 2/Lt J. McFARLANE.

9. The strictest march discipline both of dismounted personnel & transport will be maintained throughout. The transport will keep an interval of not less than 200 yards between itself & any other Unit's transport

10. ACKNOWLEDGE
    Issued by hand at 8.30 p.m.

    1. File   7. D Section
    2/3 War Diary   8. Tpt "
    4. A Section   9. C.S.M.
    5. B "   10. C.Q.M.S.
    6. C "   11. 186th Inf. Bde.

    L. Cohen
    Capt.
    Cmdg. 213th M.G. Coy

213 W. G. Coy

Appendix, p 6

Volume 12

February 1918

War Diary

213th Machine Gun Company
Daily Orders Part II

No 19 (Page 1)
14/2/18

1. To Hospital.

122972 Pte Tooth W	D	Section	To hospital	8/2/18
122183 " Bowman R	C	"	"	8/2/18
124600 " Popple A	C	"	"	12/2/18
87693 L/Cpl Clunkery S	A	"	"	14/2/18
12422 Pte Boutcher J	D	"	"	14/2/18

2. From Hospital.

121732 Pte Hemingsley J	D	"	From hospital	12/2/18

3. To Course.

64156 L/Cpl Eaton T	A	"	To gas course	9/2/18
20292 Sgt Norman H	A	"	To B.M.T.S. "	11/2/18
11289 Cpl McLean C	D	"	" "	12/2/18
25255 L/Cpl Flaxman G	C	"	" "	12/2/18
63889 " Rickard A	Trpt	"	Horse Management course	14/2/18

4. Reinforcements (Strength Increase)

127395 Pte Hicks C			From Base	7/2/18
127396 " Scrivener G			"	7/2/18
28409 " Boyd E			"	7/2/18

5. Postings.

127395 " Hicks C			To B Section	7/2/18
127396 " Scrivener G			" B "	7/2/18
28409 " Boyd E			" D "	7/2/18

6. Strength Decrease.

37022 Pte Lomas T	Trpt.	Section	To hospital Manchester whilst on leave	3/1/18
118693 " Sarkewitz A	B	"	To 42 C.C.S.	7/2/18
121752 " Hall A.H.	A	"	" 42 "	7/2/18
118071 " Kitson W	A	"	" 42 "	9/2/18
Lieut R.A.T. Miller	H.Q	"	Trfd to 171 Coy. To Command	11/2/18
57478 Pte Jordan J	H.Q	"	Trfd to 171 Coy. Batman to Lt Miller	11/2/18

7. Leave to U.K. & Ration Allowance

Lt. C.J. Eaton	B	Section	Leave to U.K.	11/2/18–25/2/18
13206 Pte Clarke G.	A	"	"	"
42893 Cpl Cunningham J	B	"	"	"
54666 L/Cpl Thornley A	C	"	"	"
3665 Pte Littlefair A	C	"	"	"

7. Leave to U.K. & Ration Allce (cont'd).   No 198 (Page 2)

64238 Pte Brown T.T.	D Section	Leave to U.K. 11/2/18 to 25/2/18
81561 " Robinson A.	D	"	"	"
63879 L/C Holloway A	Trspt	"	"	"
28385 " Jones D	"	"	"	"
64433 Pte Bamford J	"	"	"	"
64746 " Ellis E	"	"	"	"
63359 " Grafton J	"	"	"	"
64491 " O'Brien C	"	"	"	"
21656 L/C Hudson M	H.Q.	"	"	"
44365 Pte Griffiths J	H.Q.	"	"	"
81603 " Hume G	H.Q.	"	"	"

8. Promotions.

84874 A/Cpl Speed W   B   "   To be Cpl, vice Cpl Smith, to England (Auth: A.G. Jnro A 2/5/2/18).   23/1/18

9. Field Punishments & Deprivation of Pay

119,280 Pte Cooke W   D Section   not complying with an order 1/2/18   8/2/18
                                        28 days F.P. No 1

119946 " Ormisher W   C   "   not complying with an order 1/2/18   8/2/18
                                 28 days F.P. No 1

115755 " Wood J.W.   B   "   not complying with an order 1/2/18   8/2/18
                                 28 days F.P. No 1

65542 " Merrill J   B   "   Breach of march discipline 6/2/18   11/2/18
                               Deprived 3 days pay

10 Punishments

68391 L/C Broadway S   C   "   (1) Neglect of duty whilst on guard
                                  (2) not complying with   8/2/18
                                  an order — Deprived of Lance stripe

64761 " Gibson B   B   "   Neglect of duty whilst on guard 8/2/18   8/2/18
                              Reprimanded

No 19 (Page 3)

1 Infantry Attached.

26229 Pte Murray J.	A Section	From 5th Batt	D. of W.	14/2/18
205504 " Arnold G.	A "	"	"	"
241815 " Iredale J.	A "	"	"	"
205363 " Willey N.	A "	"	"	"
203604 " Berry L.	A "	"	"	"
201009 " Keech E.	B "	"	"	"
30611 " Bowers N.	B "	"	"	"
29096 " Hawley A.	B "	"	"	"
241,104 " Hall H.A.	C "	"	"	"

2 Extension of Leave.

67759 Pte Coates S.   A Section   Leave extended 8/2/18 to 13/2/18

From Leave to U.K.

67636 Sgt Twigg W.	B Section	From leave	14/2/18
54917 L/Cpl Foster P.	H.Q.	"	1.2/18
67759 Pte Coates S.	A	"	14/2/18

J. W. Garland
Lt for Capt
Cmdg. 213th M.G. Coy.

213 W. S. Coy

Appendix No 4

Volume 12

February 1918

War Diary

213. Machine Gun Company
Daily Orders Part II

N° 20 (Page 1)
21.2.18

1. <u>From Hospital</u>
121640 Pte Popple A.   C Section   From hospital   19.2.18

2. <u>Reinforcements</u>
126106 Pte Worpole A.   Joined from Base   16.2.18
128064 " Wilson S.   "   "   "   16.2.18
       Lieut Williams H.V.   Trsfd from 212 M.G.Coy 17.2.18
                                 as 2i/c authority
                                 A.Gs./57/256.

46104 Pte Trevett B.   Trsfd from 212 M.G.Coy 17.2.18

3. <u>Strength Decrease</u>
106569 Dr Black R.   Trsp t Sectn.   To 42 C.C.S.   12.2.18
103120 Pte Shelton G.   B   "   "   "   "   13.2.18
84698 Cpl Plunkett S.   A   "   "   "   "   14.2.18

4. <u>From Course</u>
11289 Cpl McLean C.   D   "   From course   16.2.18
25255 L/C Flaxman C.   C   "   "   "   16.2.18
64156 L/C Eaton F.   A   "   "   "   16.2.18
85583 Pte Carr B.   C   "   "   "   18.2.18

5. <u>To Course</u>
103042 L/C Gray H.   D   "   To Infantry course 18.2.18
20100   " Shepherd J.   C   "   "   "   "   18.2.18
82042   " Wright H.   B   "   "   "   "   18.2.18
64376 Pte Burr R.   HQ.   "   To St OMER for final
                                         trade test.   20.2.18

6. <u>Infantry attached</u>
306544 Pte Sutcliffe N. D Section   From 2/7. D of W.   15.2.18
8060   " Cunnington A. "   "   "   "   "   "   17.2.18

7. <u>Postings</u>
126106 Pte Worpole A.   To D. Section   16.2.18
128064 " Wilson S.   " A   "   16.2.18
       Lieut Williams H.V.   " H.Q   "   17.2.18
46104 Pte Trevett B.   " HQ   "   17.2.18

(P.T.O.

8. Promotions & Appointments   No 20. (Page 2)

81497. P/L/C. Hughes.A.   A. Sectn.   To be A/Cpl vice 87698
                                        Cpl Plunkett S. to
                                        hospital   14.2.18.

64156. L/L/C Eaton.F.   A   "   To be A/P/L/C vice
                                        81497 P/L/C Hughes
                                        apptd A/Cpl.   14.2.18

89624   Pte Hawker.A.   A   "   Apptd L/L/C.   20.2.18
118700   "   Turner W.   A   "   " A/L/L/C   20.2.18
58734   "   Simison W.   C   "   " L/L/C   8.2.18.

9. From Leave to U.K.
7144 Sgt. Handford.J. D Section   From Leave.   21.2.18
64406. Cpl. Down.W.   C   "   "   "   21.2.18
58734 Pte Simison W.   C   "   "   "   21.2.18
82373   " Feaviour.F. B   "   "   "   21.2.18

                                            L. Shaw   Capt.
                                        Cmdg 213 M.G. Coy.

War Diary
Supplementary

213 Machine Gun Company
Daily Orders Part II

No 20 (Page 1)
21.2.18.

1. Cancellations.
Reference Daily Orders Part 2 dated 21/2/18 Page 2 Para 8
Cancel entries relating to:-
   8mo,y Pte Hughes. W.
   64156. A/L/C. Eaton. J.
   118700 Pte. Turner W.

2. Rejoined Strength Increase
548440 Sgt. Attwood A.E.   Rejoined from Base 21.2.18

3. Reversions
87636 A/Sgt. Twigg W.   B. section   Reverts to Cpl   21.2.18
            on 548440 Sgt Attwood
            rejoining Coy.

64140 A/Cpl Down W.   C "   Reverts to U/L/C   21.2.18
            on A/Sgt Twigg reverting
            to Cpl.

4. Appointments.
64140 U/L/C Down W.   Apptd A/Cpl vice
             87698 Cpl Plunkett
             to hospital   21.2.18
87636 Cpl Twigg W.   Apptd A/L/Sgt.   21.2.18

5. Postings
548440 Sgt Attwood A.E.   To C. Section   21.2.18

6. Transfers (Inter. Section)
24053 Sgt Calfe. W.   C. Section   To B Section   21.2.18

7. From leave to U.K.
81899 Pte Akers. G.   A "   From leave   21.2.18
55881 " Rogers J.   A "   " "   21.2.18

               L. Pollak Capt.
             Cmdg 213 M.G. Coy.

2.13 W.I. Coy.

Appendix No. 8

Volume 12

February 1918

No 20 Page 2)

7. Leave to U.K. & Ration allowance

51497	L/C Hughes A.	A Section	Leave to U.K.	23.2.18 / 9.3.18
68744	Pte Swaddle J.	A	"	"
67765	" Wunford A.	A	"	"
54086	Sgt Darbyshire	B	"	"
67741	L/C Gibson B	B	"	"
64232	Pte Chamberlain	B	"	"
64233	" Fisher J	C	"	"
54919	" Nibbs B	C	"	"
67765	" Thomson C	C	"	"
68201	" Broadway S	C	"	"
81489	" Parnell P	D	"	"
67813	" Monk W	D	"	"
58695	" Wells W	D	"	"
37443	" Hutton C	Trspt	"	"
63861	L/C Greaves G	Trspt	"	"
63867	Pte Bodily C	Trspt	"	"
63882	" Fitch J	Trspt	"	"
64338	" Dean W	H.Q.	"	"
64340	L/C Buchanan E	H.Q.	"	"
55253	Pte Bracey P	H.Q.	"	"

8. Reinforcements

68002	Pte Cryan J.	Joined from Base	27.2.18
67767	" Austin R	"	27.2.18
128945	" Chattell P.	"	27.2.18
128948	" Dicker W.	"	27.2.
65547	" Haynes A.	"	27.2.

9. Postings

128945	Pte Chattell P	To A Section	27.2.18
128948	" Dicker W.	" A	27.2.18
67767	" Austin R.	" B	27.2.18
68002	" Cryan J.	" D	27.2.18
65547	" Haynes A.	" C	27.2.18

L. _____ Capt
Cmdg 213 M.G. Coy.

23rd Machine Gun Coy
Daily Orders Part II   No 81 Pg 1)
                                          23.2.18

1. To hospital
        ... Gilson   ...   To hospital   ...
   055 Cpl Birchenough C   "   "   "   26.2.18
   669 Sgt Murray J   "   To Military
                                         Hospl Halifax 20.2.18
                                         whilst on leave UK

   25406 Pte Joyce W   To hospital   27...

2. From hospital
   12185 Pte Bowman R   C scen   From hospital 20...

3. From leave
   37275 Pte Burkitt H   AA   From leave   ...
   6771   L/C McDonald A   A   "   "   22.2.18
   64493 Pte Sanford J   Trsp   "   "   26.2.18
   63819 Pte Holloway A   "   "   21.2.18
   28506 Pte Town   "   "   27.2.18
   63359 Pte Gratton J   "   "   24.2.18
          2/Lt C.S. Caton   B   "   "   26.2.18
   21565 L/C Hudson   A   "   "   26.2.18
   41325 Pte Griffiths J   "   "   "   26.2.18
   81603 "   Kerne G   "   "   "   26.2.18
   58666 "   Thornley A   C   "   "   22.2.18
   63206 "   Clark L   B   "   "   26.2.18
   42893 C/S Cummings J   B   "   "   26.2.18
   64238 Pte Brown H.J   C   "   "   26.2.18
   81501 "   Robinson A   D   "   "   26.2.18

4. To Course
   66501 Cpl Rance A   D   To AA Course   23.2.18
   81450 "   Newby W   C   Gas Course   ...

5. From Course
   63869 L/C Richard A   Trsp   From course   24.2.18

6. On Command
   34611 Pte Thornley J   To England
                                         for commission 27.2.18

213 M.G. Coy

Appendix No 5

Volume 12

February 1918

9TH DIVISION
STH AFN INFY BRIGADE

STH AFRICAN INFANTRY
JLY - DEC 1916

www.ingramcontent.com/pod-product-compliance
Lightning Source LLC
Chambersburg PA
CBHW080903230426
43664CB00016B/2718